# Lecture Notes
# in Business Information Processing     70

W0192958

Erik Proper   Marc M. Lankhorst
Marten Schönherr   Joseph Barjis
Sietse Overbeek (Eds.)

# Trends in Enterprise Architecture Research

5th International Workshop, TEAR 2010
Delft, The Netherlands, November 12, 2010
Proceedings

 Springer

Volume Editors

Erik Proper
Public Research Centre Henri Tudor
29, avenue John F. Kennedy, 1855 Luxembourg-Kirchberg, Luxembourg
E-mail: erik.proper@tudor.lu

Marc M. Lankhorst
Novay
P.O. Box 589, 7500 AN Enschede, The Netherlands
E-mail: Marc.Lankhorst@novay.nl

Marten Schönherr
Deutsche Telekom Laboratories
Ernst-Reuter-Platz 7, 10587 Berlin, Germany
E-mail: marten.schoenherr@telekom.de

Joseph Barjis
Delft University of Technology
Faculty of Technology, Policy and Management
Section of Systems Engineering
P.O. Box 5015, 2600 GA Delft, The Netherlands
E-mail: j.barjis@tudelft.nl

Sietse Overbeek
Delft University of Technology
Faculty of Technology, Policy and Management
Section of Information and Communication Technology
P.O. Box 5015, 2600 GA Delft, The Netherlands
E-mail: s.j.overbeek@tudelft.nl

Library of Congress Control Number: 2010937764

ACM Computing Classification (1998): J.1, H.3.5, H.4.1, D.2

ISSN       1865-1348
ISBN-10    3-642-16818-3 Springer Berlin Heidelberg New York
ISBN-13    978-3-642-16818-5 Springer Berlin Heidelberg New York

springer.com

© Springer-Verlag Berlin Heidelberg 2010
Printed in Germany

Typesetting: Camera-ready by author, data conversion by Scientific Publishing Services, Chennai, India
Printed on acid-free paper        06/3180      5 4 3 2 1 0

# Preface

The 2010 Workshop on Trends in Enterprise Architecture Research (TEAR), held in Delft, The Netherlands, was the fifth one in an increasingly successful series of workshops, previously held in Hong Kong, Switzerland, Australia and Sweden. This year we received 15 papers. After an extensive review process by a distinguished international Program Committee, with each paper receiving at least three reviews, we accepted the 7 papers that appear in these proceedings. Congratulations to the successful authors!

The discipline of enterprise architecture is commonly considered to have its birth in an academic article by John Zachman published by the research-oriented IBM Systems Journal. The growth of the discipline, however, took place mainly in the practitioner's cradle. In recent years, the industrial and governmental interest in enterprise architecture has increased dramatically. Meanwhile, there has been steady academic work in the area, but research on enterprise architecture has been taking place in relatively isolated communities. The main objective of this workshop was to bring these different communities of EA researchers together and to identify trends and major research challenges in EA research. This workshop provided a discussion forum where researchers and practitioners could meet and exchange experiences, problems and ideas related to EA.

This year's papers cover reports on the effectiveness of enterprise architecture, case studies, core concepts of enterprise architectures, architecture description languages, as well as papers on the software and IT aspects of enterprise architecture.

The paper by Vasilis Boucharas, Marlies van Steenbergen, Slinger Jansen, and Sjaak Brinkkemper concerns a literature survey on the potential contribution of enterprise architecture to the achievement of business goals, while the paper by Ulrik Franke, Mathias Ekstedt, Robert Lagerström, Jan Saat and Robert Winter complements this from a more practical perspective by providing a survey on the usage of enterprise architecture in practice.

The paper by Sandeep Purao and Kevin Desouza reports on a large enterprise architecture case study conducted in the United States of America.

Fundamental concepts for the field of enterprise architecture are discussed in two papers. The paper by Sabine Buckl, Florian Matthes, Sascha Roth, Christopher Schulz, and Christian M. Schweda discusses a framework of concepts for enterprise architecture design, while the paper by Erik Proper and Danny Greefhorst zooms in on the concept of architecture principles as one of the cornerstones of enterprise architecture.

The final two papers of the proceedings zoom in on software and IT aspects of enterprise architecture. The paper by Damien A. Tamburri, Patricia Lago and Henry Muccini is concerned with the role of an architecture description language for the representation of software architecture, while the paper by Helge

Buckow, Hans-Jürgen Groß, Gunther Piller, Karl Prott, Johannes Willkomm, and Alfred Zimmermann is concerned with the integration of standard platforms in heterogeneous IT landscapes.

August 2010

Erik Proper
Marc Lankhorst
Marten Schönherr
Sietse Overbeek
Joseph Barjis

# Organization

## Workshop Co-chairs

| | |
|---|---|
| Erik Proper (Chair) | Public Research Center – Henri Tudor, Luxembourg |
| Marc M. Lankhorst | Novay Enschede, The Netherlands |
| Marten Schönherr | Deutsche Telekom Laboratories, Berlin, Germany |

## Steering Committee

| | |
|---|---|
| Stephan Aier | University of St. Gallen, Switzerland |
| Pontus Johnson | KTH Royal Institute of Technology Stockholm, Sweden |
| Marc M. Lankhorst | Novay Enschede, The Netherlands |
| Joachim Schelp | University of St. Gallen, Switzerland |
| Marten Schönherr | Deutsche Telekom Laboratories, Berlin, Germany |

## Program Committee

| | |
|---|---|
| Antonia Albani | Delft University of Technology, The Netherlands |
| Elmar J. Sinz | University of Bamberg, Germany |
| Erik Proper | Radboud University Nijmegen and Capgemini, The Netherlands |
| Florian Matthes | Technical University Munich, Germany |
| Gerhard Schwabe | University of Zurich, Switzerland |
| Gerold Riempp | European Business School, Germany |
| Giuseppe Berio | University of South Brittany, France |
| Haluk Demirkan | Arizona State University, USA |
| Marc Lankhorst | Novay, The Netherlands |
| Martin Zelm | CIMOSA Association, Germany |
| Mathias Ekstedt | Royal Institute of Technology, Sweden |
| Matthias Goeken | Frankfurt School of Finance & Management, Germany |
| Michael Rosemann | Queensland University of Technology, Australia |
| Michael zur Muehlen | Stevens Institute of Technology, USA |
| Pedro Sousa | Lisbon Technical University and Link Consulting, Portugal |
| Pontus Johnson | Royal Institute of Technology, Sweden |
| Scott Bernard | Carnegie Mellon University, USA |
| Tim O'Neill | University of Technology Sydney, Australia |

| Udo Bub | Deutsche Telekom Laboratories, Germany |
| Ulrich Frank | University of Duisburg-Essen, Germany |
| Ulrike Steffens | OFFIS, Germany |
| Wilhelm Hasselbring | University of Kiel, Germany |
| Wolfgang Keller | objectarchitects, Germany |

# Table of Contents

# The Contribution of Enterprise Architecture to the Achievement of Organizational Goals: A Review of the Evidence

Vasilis Boucharas[1], Marlies van Steenbergen[2],
Slinger Jansen[1], and Sjaak Brinkkemper[1]

[1] Department of Information and Computing Sciences, Utrecht University,
Padualaan 14, 3584CH Utrecht, The Netherlands
vboucharas@gmail.com
[2] Architecture and Business Solutions, Sogeti Netherlands B.V., Postbus 76,
4130 EB Vianen, The Netherlands

**Abstract.** This paper reports the findings of a systematic review on the literature concerning the potential contribution of Enterprise Architecture (EA) to the achievement of various business goals. The review revealed the current state of the scientific and practitioner's literature concerning the potential benefits of EA as describing 29 unique contexts within which EA has been found to deliver 100 unique benefits through 3 value-generative mechanisms. This review enhances the understanding of EA of both researchers and practitioners by providing valuable information on the potential benefits of EA and their relationships, their applicability (context), and the mechanisms that generate them. Additionally, this review is expected to enable practitioners to establish the business case for EA by means of scientifically grounded reasoning about how EA might contribute to the achievement of certain business goals.

**Keywords:** enterprise architecture, organizational goals, systematic review.

## 1 Introduction

Although considered to be relatively young [1,2,3], Enterprise Architecture (EA) has generally evolved into a well-accepted discipline [3] and its importance is considered to be growing [1]. Curiously enough, to date, there exists no single comprehensive view of the ways EA might add value to an organization. This carries several implications:

Firstly, it inhibits establishing a common understanding, among practitioners and researchers alike, of the potential of EA as a discipline and how it may lead to desirable organizational outcomes [4]. As a consequence, comparisons to other, already established business governance instruments become difficult and ambiguity is introduced over the specific value proposition of EA.

Secondly, it inhibits the establishment of the business case for EA due to the difficulty of demonstrating the business value of the project at hand. Slot, Dedene,

E. Proper et al. (Eds.): TEAR 2010, LNBIP 70, pp. 1–15, 2010.

and Maes find it surprising that to a large extent, the business case for the current EA activities that take place in the business and IT world is non-existent [5]. Increasingly, traditional cost-justification methods are found to be inappropriate for measuring the contribution of IS/IT investments in general [6]. More specifically, quantifying the value of EA is considered to be a challenge [2,7] and research strictly focusing on financial benefits is considered to represent a very limited view [3]. The alternative is to make use of contribution-justification. In this respect though, the absence of a comprehensive, scientifically grounded framework of potential EA benefits inhibits establishing the business case for EA. Finally, it inhibits the establishment of standardized and reusable technical EA effectiveness metrics since the entire breadth of the indirect effects of EA is not known.

Although on the whole the (mostly practitioner-oriented) literature displays an abundance of potential EA benefits, these are mostly inconsistently scientifically grounded [4]. Even in those cases that the EA benefits are consistently and scientifically grounded, they are usually presented as being under the direct influence of the architectural practice, lacking any justification as far as the cause and effect relationships between them, the EA practice, and the ultimate business goals are concerned. However, Steenbergen and Brinkkemper [3] conducted several relevant exploratory case studies and found that in reality, the nature and complexity of the cause and effect relationships occurring between multiple differencing benefits is far more indirect and complicated.

In this first in a series of upcoming research papers reporting on the establishment of a comprehensive, scientifically grounded framework of potential EA benefits, we present a systematic review of the evidence regarding the effectiveness of EA. With the goal of researching not only the benefits of EA, but equally important, the cause and effect relationship chains between them, and in order to maximize the richness and depth of the analysis of the evidence, we apply the design-oriented research synthesis method proposed by Denyer et al. [8], an extension of Pawson's *realist synthesis* method [9]. Using this method we extract *design propositions* (or technological rules [10]) in the lines of the Context Intervention Mechanism Outcome (CIMO) logic [8]. For Aken, a technological rule is a fragment of general knowledge (or general solution) that in a specific field of application links an intervention or an artifact with some expected outcome or performance [11]. Denyer et al. similarly see a design proposition as offering a general template for creating solutions for a specific class of problems [8].

A design proposition made up of CIMO-logic components is formed in principle as follows: for some problematic Context(s), use some specific Intervention(s) that will invoke some generative Mechanism(s) that in turn will deliver the desired Outcome(s). Design propositions thus not only inform on what to do in a specific situation in order to create a specific effect but more importantly, they offer some insight on why it happens [8].

In Section 2 we describe the literature review methodology. In Section 3 we present the findings of the review in terms of Context, Mechanism and Outcome elements as well as by applying a model, the Enterprise Architecture Benefits Map (EABM), for documenting, structuring and making sense of the Outcomes (or EA Benefits) and their relationships. In Section 4 we discuss the findings, their implications, and we propose future research. We conclude in Section 5.

## 2   Research Method

For the literature review we followed the Systematic Literature Review (SLR) methodology of Tranfield et al. [12]. The authors propose a methodology for conducting SLRs pertinent to the management research domain by transposing relevant, established and highly influential methodologies from the medical research domain (i.e. [13,14]). The rationale for adopting such a highly structured and systematic methodology lies in maximizing rigor, minimizing bias, and enhancing the traceability and reproducibility of the results. In this line, certain enhancements were applied to certain process steps of the SLR methodology by extending them with methodological adaptations from the *Cochrane Handbook for Systematic Reviews of Interventions* [13].

The review begun with identifying the need for a review and a small scoping study for acquiring a broad idea of the available literature, relevant search engines, appropriate keywords, etc. A review proposal was produced and a review panel of experienced researchers and practitioners in the field of EA was assembled with the aim of resolving disputes. Departing from Tranfield et al., and along the guidelines for review protocol construction presented in the Cochrane Handbook, a protocol was developed for laying down the methods/guidelines for conducting the review.

The following seven search engines were searched: Science Citation Index, The ACM Guide, IEEE CSDL, CiteSeerX, Emerald, Elsevier/Science Direct, and EBSCO. We retrieved 613 results from all search engines. Judging by the title and abstract, 543 contributions were found to be duplicates or obviously irrelevant. To compensate for the mechanistic approach of the systematic review, 19 contributions were added from the researchers' personal collection of studies and another 18 contributions from examining the references of other contributions. In total, 107 contributions remained for full-text review.

*Studies Quality Assessment.* Two types of criteria for considering studies for this review were developed. The first relates to an evaluation of the eligibility of the study type and the second to an evaluation of a study's inner quality aspects. Eligible study types were considered to be quantitative, qualitative, and mixed-method scholarly research and *gray literature* (i.e. literature that has not been formally published) in an effort to capture the broadest possible definitions of EA benefits. Inclusion of gray literature to systematic reviews is considered to be advantageous in order to help minimize publication bias effects [15,16].

For qualitatively evaluating the studies, we adopted a *post-positivism*[1] standpoint. More specifically, we constructively embraced the *subtle-realism* philosophy [18] which advocates that quantitative and qualitative research can be

---

[1] Post-positivism is associated with those researchers that advocate the use of the same broad criteria for evaluating all research types [17].

qualitatively assessed using the same broad concepts of validity and relevance, but operationalized differently [19]. Both relevance and validity reflect common, recurring research evaluation criteria in the scientific literature (e.g. [17,18] and [17,20] respectively). In operationalizing the validity and relevance concepts we developed a set of common screening questions as well as separate criteria lists for quantitative (adapting the list appearing in [21]) and qualitative (adapting lists appearing in [22,23,19]) studies.

In line with other researchers' views, and as a *realist synthesis* approach for the data synthesis was adopted, every contribution was additionally judged based on its "fit for purpose" [24], whether it added anything important to our understanding of the phenomenon under review [25], and on its quality as it was established in relation to the rest of the contributions of the synthesis [26]. Thus, highly relevant and original contributions were included in the review even if they displayed certain quality issues.

During the full-text review 6 contributions were found to have invalid study types and 68 were found to be irrelevant to the synthesis; these were subsequently removed. During the synthesis of the remaining 33 studies, 19 were removed based on qualitative issues. In total, 14 studies were included in the synthesis: [1,4,27,28,29,30,31,32,33,34,35,36,37,38].

*Synthesis Methodology.* For the data extraction and synthesis, we conformed to the CIMO-logic categories proposed by Denyer et al. [8], described above. Adjusting the CIMO-logic to this research's goals, we extracted and synthesized data into the following categories:

(C) contexts for which EA has been found to be of value,
(I) EA as the sole intervention of interest,
(M) mechanisms that answer how or why EA produces or contributes, directly or indirectly, to certain organizational outcomes, and
(O) organizational outcomes-results of the application of EA (alternatively referred upon as *EA Benefits*).

The 14 eligible contributions that were processed with CIMO-logic had their data extracted into appropriate electronic extraction forms created in a commercial RDBMS. Data was extracted by the principal researcher only. No ambiguities occurred, so the Review Panel was not called for resolving any disputes at this stage. In total, 163 CIMO Elements and 181 CIMO Elements Relationships were extracted. Next, those CIMO Elements that were deemed to be semantically equivalent were merged in order to create a list of unique CIMO Elements. After the merge, remained in total 133 Unique CIMO Elements and 168 Unique CIMO Elements Relationships.

It is important to note that not all CIMO Relationships reflect cause and effect relationships. A relationship between a Context and EA (the Intervention) suggests that EA has been found to be of value in the specific Context; between EA and a Mechanism, suggests that EA has been found to invoke/realize the specific Mechanism; between EA or a Mechanism, and an Outcome, suggests indeed a cause and effect relationship between them: the Outcome being the result of the application/introduction of the EA or the Mechanism.

# 3   Results

We begin by presenting an overview of the most important (for brevity reasons) Context themes identified in the included studies. Where they exist, the Relationships of the Contexts with other elements (i.e. the EA, EA Mechanisms, and Outcomes) are described in-text. We then present the EA Mechanisms identified in the included studies, which are given in their entirety since we were only able to locate scarce evidence along three studies. We also textually describe existing Relationships between EA Mechanisms and other elements (i.e. Contexts, EA, and Outcomes). Finally, with the aid of the EABM, we graphically present an overview of the Outcomes and some Relationships, as identified in the included studies.

A complete account of the CIMO Elements and their Relationships, along with a description when necessary, is provided in [39]. For a better understanding of the nature of the individual elements the reader is strongly advised to refer to the original studies.

## Contexts for Which EA Has Been Found to Be of Value (C)

*Organizational Design.* EA has been found to provide the necessary support in the context of organizational design problems. These problems might relate to the design of new organizational structures [37] or the re-design of existing ones, during mergers and acquisitions [36,1], and during general organizational change and restructuring [31,34]. In designing new organizational structures specifically, and in the context of an action research study by Arnold, Op 't Land, and Dietz [37], EA was reported to enable the communication of project investment decisions, to enable the conceptual consolidation of a project's to-be situation between stakeholders, and to support project scoping.

*Project Portfolio Management.* EA has been found to provide support in the context of Project Portfolio Management, in cases like project portfolio planning [1], IT portfolio management [36], and in addition in related investment decisions [36].

*Decision Making.* EA has been found to aid in the context of general decision-making [36] activities, as well as in making decisions relating to Sourcing [1] and the adoption of COTS Software [1].

*Regulatory Compliance.* EA has been found to provide support in the context of regulatory compliance, be it general compliance management [1] or quality management [1].

*Systems Development.* EA has been found to be of help in the context of Systems Development, from the first phases during Project Initialization (e.g. project scoping) [1] to general Systems Development support [36].

*Risk Management.* EA has been proposed to aid in the context of Risk Management. Although there were cases identified were EA has been found to assist in Business Continuity Planning [1] most of the risk management scenarios identified were IT-related; ranging from Security Management [1], Technology Risk

Management [1], and IT Service Management [1], to more specific cases of integrated Security Management solutions in business networks with heterogeneous ICT [29]. In the latter, and in the context of a single case study, Pulkkinen, Naumenko, and Luostarinen [29] report that EA contributes to a number of Outcomes, like increasing the inter-organizational transparency and security of exchanges of information and services, and ensuring the comprehensive and coordinated IT and Security Management and Planning.

*IT Costs Reduction.* EA has also been found to be supportive in the context of reducing IT-related costs, either through IT Consolidation (e.g. by eliminating costly, redundant technological platforms) [1] or by better Management of IT operations costs [1].

*Organization Type.* There has been some evidence concerning the applicability of EA in both public and private organizations. Gregor, Hart, and Martin [33] reported in the context of a study of an Australian government organization that the application of EA was found to contribute to a number of Outcomes and ultimately to that of Business and IT alignment, partially as a result of introducing the EA Mechanism *IS/IT Governance Framework*. Similarly, Martin, Gregor, and Hart [38] reported in the context of a study of two Australian government organizations that the application of EA was also found to contribute to a number of Outcomes and ultimately to that of Business and IT alignment (or business processes and IS alignment). Finally, Kamogawa and Okada [30] deal with the business value of EA for private organizations in the context of a survey of 300 stock-exchange-listed Japanese companies. Notably, their study addresses, among others, the unearthing of a positive correlation between various financial measurements (e.g. ROA, ROS) which reflect an improvement in business performance and the application of EA.

## EA Mechanisms That Generate Outcomes (M)

*EA Standards.* In the context of a firm-level survey of 90 respondents that represent large and geographically dispersed organizations with subunits with considerable autonomy in IT resources management, Boh and Yellin [32] reported on the significant effect of EA Standards on reducing the IT infrastructure's components heterogeneity and services replication, and on achieving better integration of enterprise applications and data.

*EA Models.* In the context of a relatively small survey of 51 respondents, Bucher et al. [1] reported on a multitude of Contexts (or application scenarios, e.g. Security Management, IT Service Management) along four industry sectors (manufacturing, telecom, finance/insurance, and software/IT) that EA Models are said to support or constitute the foundation of.

*IS/IT Governance Framework.* In a context previously explicated, Gregor et al. [33] reported, among others, on the important contribution of an IS/IT Governance Framework to the achievement of Business and IT alignment. Beyond the scope of this research's theme, but very important nevertheless to note, is that Gregor et al. reinforce with their study the notion of the EA *contribution* towards specific goals (in this case, alignment), in combination with—and not in isolation from—other organizational alignment mechanisms.

### The Enterprise Architecture Benefits Map

In this section we briefly present the Enterprise Architecture Benefits Map (EABM), a full account of which is provided in [39]. The EABM serves as a visual-oriented model to provide and enforce an appropriate structure on the EA Benefits and their Relationships, so that they can be effectively and efficiently understood and utilized. It could be argued that the sheer number and complexity of the EA Benefits and their Relationships alone could provide the raison d'être for devising such an artifact. Furthermore, we argue that, although a "traditional" synthesis can be effective in presenting the originating studies in relation to their researched outcomes, maintaining a narrative account of the relationships between the outcomes can be cumbersome and counter-intuitive. The EABM does not represent a novel artifact but rather builds on Kaplan and Norton's Strategy Maps (SM) [40]. As such, the EABM structurally echoes, but semantically differs in certain aspects from the SM.

The EABM is comprised of four main Perspectives, each of which consists of a number of Categories, which can be thought of as the second-level logical grouping of EA Benefits. In antithesis to the SM, and for reasons of semantic consistency, no Perspective directly groups EA Benefits; instead all EA Benefits are grouped in Categories.

*The Financial Perspective.* Consists of the Financial Outcome Benefit Category, which is used to describe how various financial-related organizational EA Benefits contribute to the achievement of possibly *multiple* financial-related strategies. Financial Outcome Benefits relate to financial-related organizational outcomes including, but not limited to, financial gains occurring in relation to or as a result of the i) more effective use and re-use of artifacts, processes or other resources, ii) increase in profit or similar financial indicators, iii) reduction in costs and wasted resources.

*The Customer Perspective.* Consists of the Customer Outcome Benefit Category, which is used to describe how various customer-value-related organizational EA Benefits contribute to the achievement of possibly *multiple* customer-value-related strategies. Customer Outcome Benefits relate to customer-value-related organizational outcomes referring either to a customer-value objective achieved or to the contributing effect on such an objective. Additionally, they can relate to the i) achievement of or the contributing effect on a customer-value-related strategy, ii) realization/attainment of or contributing effect on a strategically important customer characteristic (e.g. customer group).

*The Internal Perspective.* Used to describe the various business process benefits–results of implementing an EA program on internal business processes. It

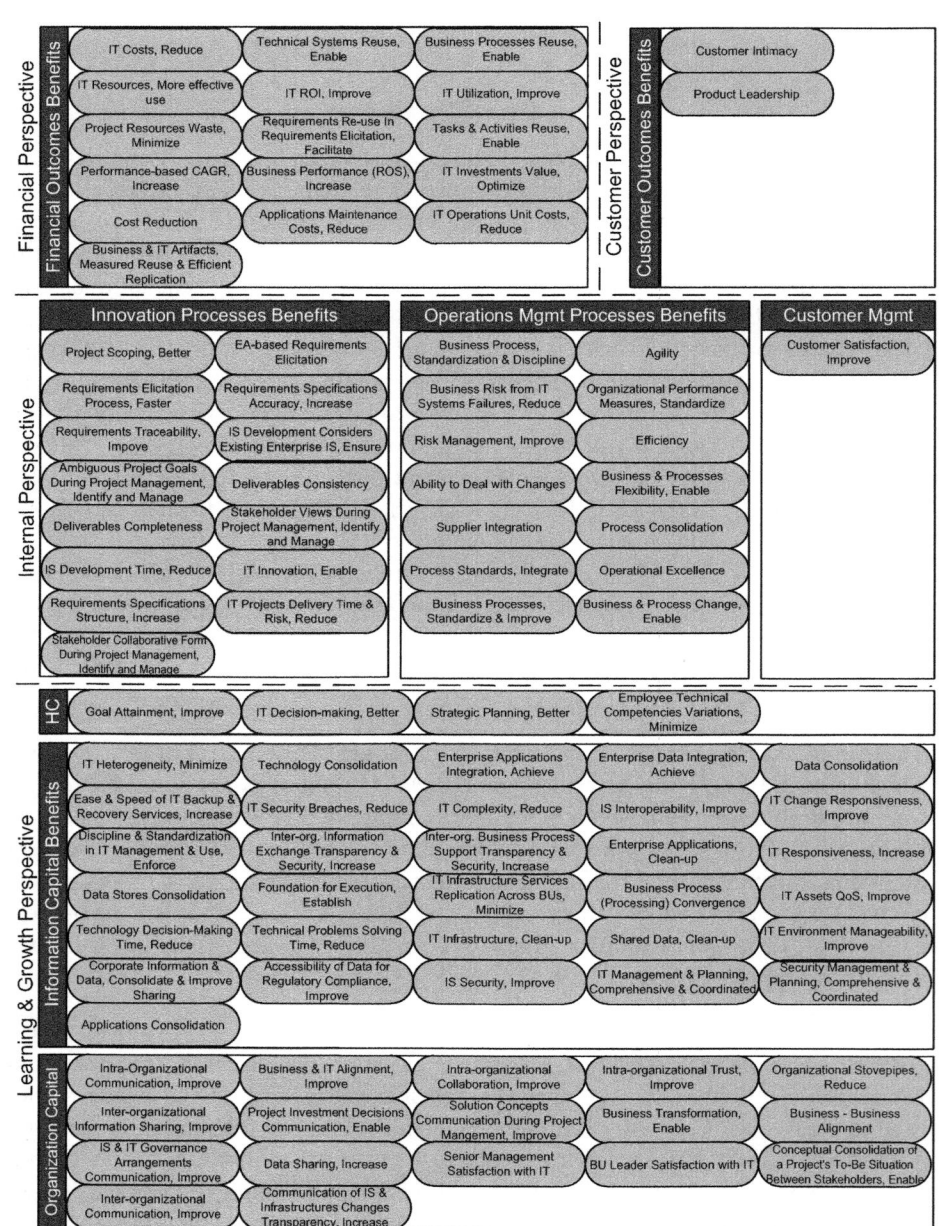

**Fig. 1.** EABM displaying all EA Benefits

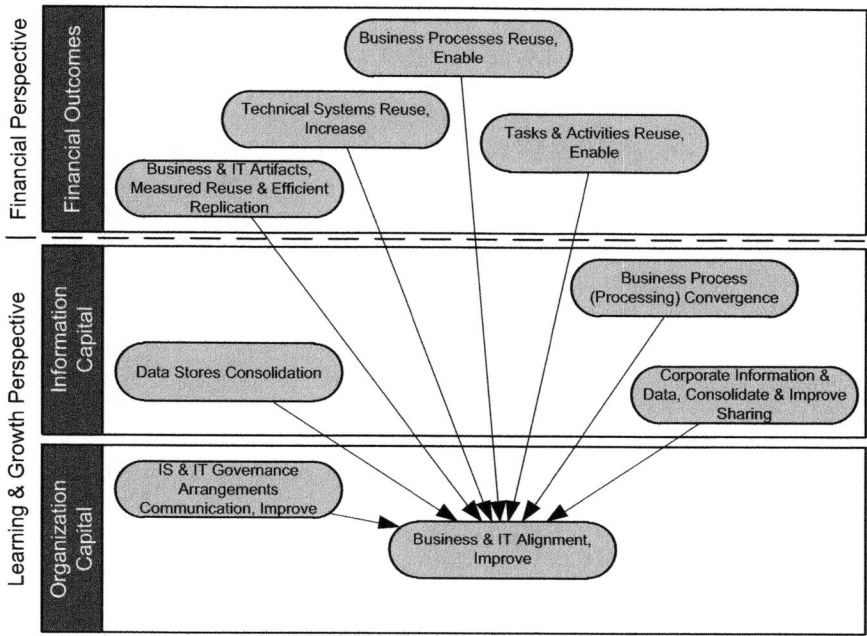

**Fig. 2.** EABM displaying those EA Benefits that directly contribute to the *Improvement of Business-IT Alignment*

consists of four Categories that group benefits stemming from the implementation of an EA program to processes relating to: i) *Operations Management Processes Category*—the production and delivery of an organization's products and services; ii) the *Customer Management Processes Category*—customer acquisition and customer relationship sustainment and growth; iii) the *Innovation Processes Category*—product/service/process innovation through R&D programs; and iv) the *Regulatory & Social Processes Category*—the management and reporting of organizational performance on national and/or local regulations, and other aspects of social interest.

*The Learning & Growth Perspective.* Used to describe those various intangible asset benefits–results of implementing an EA program on the intangible assets of an organization, and how these benefits contribute to the achievement of possibly *multiple* organizational strategies. It consists of three Categories which group benefits stemming from the implementation of an EA program to intangible assets relating to: i) the *Human Capital Category*—an organization's stock of workforce competencies; ii) the *Information Capital Category*—IT infrastructure and information capital applications; and iii) the *Organization Capital Category*—culture, leadership, teamwork and knowledge sharing, and alignment (in the EABM, *alignment* applies to individual employees towards BU and/or strategic objectives and incentives, between individual employees, and between inter/intra-organizational structures).

**Organizational Outcomes-Results of the Application of EA (O)**

After assigning the EA Benefits to the EABM categorization scheme, we drew the actual EABM (Figure 1). We observe that the majority of the EA Benefits belong to the Learning & Growth (52%) and the Internal (30%) Perspectives. The Financial Perspective ranks third (16%), and the Customer Perspective appears extremely underrepresented (2%). From the 52 EA Benefits of the Learning & Growth Perspective, almost two thirds belong to the Information Capital Category (60%), exactly one third to the Organizational Capital Category (33%), and just 8% to the Human Capital Category. From the 30 Internal Perspective EA Benefits, half belong to the Innovation Processes Category, almost all of the other half (47%) to the Operations Management Processes Category, only one belongs to the Customer Management Processes Category (3%), and none to the Regulatory & Social Processes Category. All of the 15 Innovation Processes Category's EA Benefits belong to its Design & Development Subcategory. Similarly, most of the Operations Management Processes' EA Benefits belong to its Produce Products & Services Subcategory.

In total, we identified 65 Relationships between EA Benefits. As an example, and for brevity and readability reasons, we limit ourselves in providing a second EABM (Figure 2) that displays only a subset of them: those EA Benefits that directly contribute to the Improvement of Business-IT Alignment[2].

## 4   Discussion

*Major Findings & Quality of the Evidence.* Our research results provide a rich, consolidated and scientifically established picture of the potential organizational benefits of EA. By *rich,* we mean a full account of the available research findings: unlike similar research on EA benefits (e.g. [4,41]) that reported on EA benefits without taking into account any relevant context, this research sought to understand and report not only the context within which certain benefits appear as results of the application of an EA program on an organizational structure, but also the generative mechanisms of EA that cause them.

The analysis of the 14 eligible studies revealed the current state of the scientific and practitioner's literature concerning the potential benefits of EA, as describing 29 unique contexts within which EA has been found to deliver value, 100 unique benefits of EA, and 3 mechanisms that generate the value of EA. The analysis of the results in relevant themes pinpointed, among other issues, the evident emphasis of those studies towards IT and IT-related issues, both in terms of Contexts and Outcomes—benefits of EA.

Certain contexts and several benefits have been found to semantically overlap or to group more than one notion. Some benefits could arguably pose as application scenarios (contexts) and vice versa. Others might appear vague or of high-level abstraction. These facts are characteristic of the different intentions of the original studies' authors. The "affected" elements were incorporated with the

---

[2] A complete account of the Relationships is available at [39].

rest of the results without any alterations since that could potentially introduce a range of issues from semantic discrepancies to non-existent cause and effect relationships.

The vast majority of the potentially relevant studies we located was finally excluded from the synthesis, primarily because approximately two out of three were found to be irrelevant, and secondarily because the remaining relevant studies displayed various methodological or other qualitative "deficiencies" against the assessment questions. We hold these results as indicative of the absence of a sufficient number of research programs being conducted on the effectiveness of EA, and additionally, of the relatively poor quality standards of either the contributing research or its reporting; at least as these score against the SLR's assessment questions.

Additionally, our results suggest an almost equal number of qualitative and quantitative research designs among the eligible studies. We believe though that the quantitative research design is not the most appropriate for researching and reporting rich, highly contextual evidence. For that, we hold these results as supportive to the notion of a deficit on the relative amount of rich evidence available from the eligible studies. Supportive evidence to the last claim comes from the large number of IO-logic design propositions found (in addition to CIO-, CIM-, and CI-logic ), as compared to the small number of CIMO-logic design propositions found, which is a clear indication of the relatively shallow depth of analysis undertaken in several studies. This last effect was nevertheless expected; it has been acknowledged by other researchers as it appears to be a common characteristic of the research conducted in the management domain [8].

*Meaning & Importance of the Major Findings.* The results of this research project respond to recent calls for research, not only on the potential benefits of EA [4] but–equally important–on the relationships among them [41]. This study however delivers additional value in that it takes into consideration the context in which EA benefits occur and the mechanisms through which the benefits are generated.

For the problem of defining the applicability of EA as an organizational problem-solving tool, relating EA benefits with a specific context functions as a heuristic for minimizing the problem space. Additionally, relating EA benefits with specific mechanisms of EA that generate them, provides an answer on how the benefits were actually brought about and offers an additional, critical layer of understanding of the applicability of EA.

*Overall Completeness & Applicability of the Evidence.* We hold our results as providing a competent amount of evidence regarding the identification of the benefits of EA, as these are perceived or established by researchers and practitioners of the field. The evidence put forth by the review, however, is only transferable to the extent that the individual, eligible studies' results are. The results of the literature review should be seen as *potential* benefits of EA and their realization in real-world scenarios might depend on many other contextual factors that require careful examination. Additionally, we acknowledge that there might exist other EA benefits, not yet explored in research.

The results of the SLR carry several implications for both researchers and practitioners: i) enhancing the understanding on EA by providing valuable information on potential EA benefits and their relationships, their applicability (context), and their generative mechanisms, ii) enabling the scientifically grounded reasoning on how EA might contribute to the achievement of certain business goals, establishing thus the business case for EA and EA projects, and iii) providing an extensive list of EA benefits that can function as a source for defining relevant objectives for EA programs, as well as for defining EA effectiveness metrics.

*Potential Biases & Limitations in the Review Process.* The SLR method utilized enabled a highly structured process with transparent and traceable results: all aspects of the evidence produced and the relevant rationale that produced them, are readily available and reported in [39]. However, the studies' eligibility compliance was undertaken solely by the main researcher. To counter possible bias, ambiguities were resolved after consulting with members of the review panel.

In addition, although the study contends to be highly inclusive regarding the total number of available studies on the subject of EA effectiveness, we understand that it is highly improbable to have located all of them with the reported search process, for a number of good reasons. First, we expect additional studies to be available in other languages than the one our search focused on (English). Second, we expect more gray literature to exist in sources that the researchers do not currently have access to or are unaware of (e.g. organizational statistics, internal reports). Third, we excluded search keywords relating to and studies specifically reporting on the effects of Service Oriented Architecture (SOA), as we have found the relationship between EA and SOA to be currently vaguely—and sometimes even contradictory—defined in the relevant literature. Since SOA has been defined (among others) as a competitor or an alternative to EA [42], it follows that any reported benefits of SOA cannot be readily claimed by EA.

*Suggestions for Further Research.* We propose that additional systematic reviews are conducted in the future with the aim of locating multilingual contributions and additional gray literature. Judging by the results of this SLR, it is only natural to call for more original, rigorously designed, executed, and reported research on the ways EA contributes to the achievement of specific organizational goals. Additionally, we invite researchers to make use of the EABM as a tool for charting the existing academic research, in order to identify prominent or currently uninvestigated organizational domains.

Furthermore, we propose that future research targeting the benefits of EA, might utilize the CIMO-logic prism in an effort to create useful, rich evidence that successfully relates outcomes to specific contexts and generative mechanisms; breaking thus away from the sterile IO-logic usually purported in the management domain.

# 5   Conclusion

In the context of this research we conducted a systematic review of the literature relating to the effectiveness of EA, with the explicit goal to discover those ways that the EA has been found to contribute to organizational goals. With the aid of the CIMO-logic prism for extracting design propositions from the eligible studies, and the EABM for making sense of EA Benefits and their Relationships, the review produced rich evidence on the effectiveness of EA and at the same time revealed the current state of the relevant literature. Insights gained include an evident emphasis of the existing research targeting IT and IT-related effects of EA, an evident shortage of research programs being generally conducted on the issue, an apparent poor research design and/or reporting quality of several literature contributions, and an apparent "shallow" research evidence depth— to an extent the result of the quantitative research design focus of several studies. However, we acknowledge that the study might not have covered the entire span of available literature for a number of reasons (e.g. the language of the retrieved publications).

# References

1. Bucher, T., Fischer, R., Kurpjuweit, S., Winter, R.: Enterprise architecture analysis and application: An exploratory study. In: EDOC Workshop TEAR (2006)
2. Schelp, J., Stutz, M.: A balanced scorecard approach to measure the value of enterprise architecture. In: 2nd Workshop on Trends in Enterprise Architecture Research Via Nova Architectura, pp. 5–11 (2007)
3. Steenbergen, M.v., Brinkkemper, S.: Modeling the contribution of enterprise architecture practice to the achievement of business goals. In: 17th International Conference on Information Systems Development (2008)
4. Kappelman, L., McGinnis, T., Pettite, A., Sidorova, A.: Enterprise architecture: Charting the territory for academic research. In: 14th Americas Conference on Information Systems, University of North Texas (2008)
5. Slot, R., Dedene, G., Maes, R.: Business value of solution architecture. Advances in Enterprise Engineering II, vol. 28, pp. 84–108. Springer, Heidelberg (2009)
6. Martinsons, M., Davison, R., Tse, D.: The balanced scorecard: a foundation for the strategic management of information systems. Decis. Support Syst. 25(1), 71–88 (1999)
7. Lankhorst, M.: Enterprise Architecture at Work: Modeling, Communication and Analysis. Springer, Heidelberg (December 2005)
8. Denyer, D., Tranfield, D., van Aken, J.E.: Developing design propositions through research synthesis. Organ. Stud. 29(3), 393 (2008)
9. Pawson, R.: Evidence-based policy: the promise of realist synthesis. Evaluation 8(3), 340 (2002)
10. Bunge, M.: Technology as applied science. Technol. Cult. 7(3), 329–347 (1966)
11. Aken, J.E.v.: Management research as a design science: Articulating the research products of mode 2 knowledge production in management. Br. J. Manag. 16(1), 19–36 (2005)
12. Tranfield, D.R., Denyer, D., Smart, P., Bedfordshire, M.K., Cranfield, M.K.: Towards a methodology for developing evidence-informed management knowledge by means of systematic review. Br. J. Manag. 14, 207–222 (2003)
13. Higgins, J.P.T., Green, S.: Cochrane Handbook for Systematic Reviews of Interventions. 5.0.1 edn. The Cochrane Collaboration (2008)

14. Centre for Reviews & Dissemination: Systematic Reviews: CRD's Guidance for Undertaking Reviews in Healthcare. Centre for Reviews & Dissemination, University of York, York (2009)
15. Hopewell, S., McDonald, S., Clarke, M., Egger, M.: Grey literature in meta-analyses of randomized trials of health care interventions. Cochrane Database of Systematic Reviews (2) (2007)
16. Dickersin, K., Scherer, R., Lefebvre, C.: Systematic reviews: Identifying relevant studies for systematic reviews. Br. Manag. J. 309(6964), 1286–1291 (1994)
17. Murphy, E., Dingwall, R., Greatbatch, D., Parker, S., Watson, P.: Qualitative research methods in health technology assessment: a review of the literature. Health Tech. Assess 2(16), 1–274 (1998)
18. Hammersley, M.: Reading ethnographic research: A critical guide. Longman Publishing Group, Berlin (1991)
19. Mays, N., Pope, C.: Assessing quality in qualitative research. Br. Med. J. 320(7226), 50–52 (2000)
20. Yin, R.K.: Case study research: design and methods. Sage Publications, Thousand Oaks (2003)
21. Health Care Practice Research & Development Unit, U.o.S.: Evaluation tool for quantitative research studies (2005)
22. CASP: The critical appraisal skills programme (casp): 10 questions to help you make sense of qualitative research
23. Campbell, R., Pound, P., Pope, C., Britten, N., Pill, R., Morgan, M., Donovan, J.: Evaluating meta-ethnography: a synthesis of qualitative research on lay experiences of diabetes and diabetes care. Soc. Sci. Med. 56(4), 671–684 (2003)
24. Boaz, A., Ashby, D.: Fit for purpose?: assessing research quality for evidence based policy and practice. ESRC UK Centre for Evidence Based Policy and Practice (2003)
25. Pawson, R.: Evidence-based policy: in search of a method. Evaluation 8(2), 157 (2002)
26. Pawson, R., Greenhalgh, T., Harvey, G., Walshe, K.: Realist review-a new method of systematic review designed for complex policy interventions. J. Health Serv. Res. Policy 10(1), 21–34 (2005)
27. Ross, J.W., Weill, P.: Understanding the benefits of enterprise architecture. CISR Research Briefings (2005)
28. Engelsman, W., Iacob, M.E., Franken, H.M.: Architecture-driven requirements engineering. In: 24th Annual ACM Symposium on Applied Computing, pp. 285–286. ACM, New York (2009)
29. Pulkkinen, M., Naumenko, A., Luostarinen, K.: Managing information security in a business network of machinery maintenance services business - enterprise architecture as a coordination tool. J. Syst. Softw. 80(10), 1607–1620 (2007)
30. Kamogawa, T., Okada, H.: Enterprise architecture create business value. In: 9th Annual International Symposium on Applications and the Internet, pp. 205–208 (2009)
31. Nilsson, A.: Management of technochange in an interorganizational e-government project. In: Proceedings of the 41st Annual Hawaii International Conference on System Sciences, p. 209 (2008)
32. Boh, W.F., Yellin, D.: Using enterprise architecture standards in managing information technology. J. Manag. Inform. Syst. 23(3), 163–207 (2007)
33. Gregor, S., Hart, D., Martin, N.: Enterprise architectures: enablers of business strategy and is/it alignment in government. Inform. Tech. People 20(2), 96 (2007)

34. Obitz, T., Babu, M.K.: Enterprise architecture expands its role in strategic business transformation: Infosys enterprise architecture survey 2008/2009. Technical report (2009)
35. Varnus, J., Panaich, N.: Togaf 9 enterprise architecture survey results. In: 23rd Enterprise Architecture Practitioners Conference (2009)
36. Schekkerman, J.: Trends in enterprise architecture 2005: How are organizations progressing? Technical report (2009)
37. Arnold, B., Land, M.O., Dietz, J.L.G.: Effects of an architectural approach to the implementation of shared service centers. In: 2nd International Workshop on Enterprise Applications and Services in the Finance Industry (2005)
38. Martin, N., Gregor, S., Hart, D.: Advances in Government Enterprise Architecture. In: Government Enterprise Architectures: Enabling the Alignment of Business Processes and Information Systems. Information Science Reference - Imprint, pp. 409–437. IGI Publishing, Hershey (2008)
39. Boucharas, V., Steenbergen, M.v., Jansen, S., Brinkkemper, S.: The contribution of enterprise architecture to the achievement of organizational goals: Establishing the enterprise architecture benefits framework. Technical Report UU-CS-2010-014, Department of Information and Computing Sciences, Utrecht University (2010)
40. Kaplan, R.M., Norton, D.: Strategy maps: converting intangible assets into tangible outcomes. Harvard Business School Press, Boston (2004)
41. Niemi, E.: Enterprise architecture benefits: Perceptions from literature and practice. In: 7th IBIMA Conference on the Internet & Information Systems in the Digital Age, pp. 14–16 (2006)
42. Noran, O., Bernus, P.: Service oriented architecture vs. enterprise architecture: Competition or synergy? In: Meersman, R., Tari, Z., Herrero, P. (eds.) OTM-WS 2008. LNCS, vol. 5333, pp. 304–312. Springer, Heidelberg (2008)

# Trends in Enterprise Architecture Practice – A Survey

Ulrik Franke[1], Mathias Ekstedt[1], Robert Lagerström[1],
Jan Saat[2], and Robert Winter[2]

[1] Industrial Information and Control Systems, Royal Institute of Technology,
Osquldas väg 10, 10044 Stockholm, Sweden
{ulrikf,mek101,robertl}@ics.kth.se
[2] Institute of Information Management, University of St Gallen,
Mueller-Friedberg-Strasse 8, 9000 St Gallen, Switzerland
{jan.saat,robert.winter}@unisg.ch

**Abstract.** In recent years, Enterprise Architecture (EA) has become a discipline for business and IT-system management. While much research focuses on theoretical contributions related to EA, very few studies use statistical tools to analyze empirical data.

This paper investigates the actual application of EA, by giving a broad overview of the usage of enterprise architecture in Swedish, German, Austrian and Swiss companies. 162 EA professionals answered a survey originally focusing on the relation between IT/business alignment (ITBA) and EA. The dataset provides answers to questions such as: For how many years have companies been using EA models, tools, processes and roles? How is ITBA in relation to EA perceived at companies?

In particular, the survey has investigated quality attributes of EA, related to IT-systems, business and IT governance. One important result is some interesting correlations between how these qualities are prioritized. For example, a high concern for interoperability correlates with a high concern for maintainability.

**Keywords:** Enterprise architecture, Survey, Practice, Trends.

## 1 Introduction

Managing IT-systems today is a complex business [1]. In recent years, Enterprise Architecture (EA) has become a discipline for business and IT-system management [1]. EA describes the fundamental artifacts of business and IT as well as their interrelationships [1,2,3,4,5]. Architecture models constitute the core of the approach and serve the purpose of making the complexities of the real world understandable and manageable to stakeholders [3]. A main concept in EA is the metamodel, which acts as a pattern for the instantiation of the architectural models. In other words, a metamodel is a language representation used when creating models [2,4,6,7]. EA ideally aids the stakeholders of the enterprise to effectively plan, design, document, and communicate IT and business related issues, i.e. they provide decision support for the stakeholders [7].

E. Proper et al. (Eds.): TEAR 2010, LNBIP 70, pp. 16–29, 2010.

In research EA is increasing in visibility and the strengths are frequently discussed. One question that has not been thoroughly addressed is the actual extent to which EA is employed in the industry and how this usage looks. Many research papers focus on theoretical contributions related to EA. Some use case studies to exemplify or test their EA contributions, but very few use statistical tools to test hypotheses related to EA. Thus, it is difficult to find any proof of EA really being applicable. This might be due to the fact that few companies actually employ EA today, or it may be a sign of the immaturity of the discipline. This paper does not provide this kind of proof either, however it does give some empirical input for discussion and other researchers might find interesting hypotheses to test in their work.

The contribution of this paper is twofold. Firstly, this paper aims at giving a broad overview of the usage of enterprise architecture in Swedish, German, Austrian and Swiss companies. 162 EA professionals answered a survey originally focusing on the relation between IT/business alignment (ITBA) and EA. While the results have been employed elsewhere in efforts to create actionable artifacts to achieve high ITBA [8,9], the dataset can also be used in a more descriptive fashion to answer questions such as: For how many years have companies been using EA models, tools, processes and roles? How is ITBA in relation to EA perceived at companies? How are IT-system, business and IT governance concerns perceived and prioritized at companies?

Secondly, the survey presented in this paper focused on IT/business alignment and its relation to different quality attributes of enterprise architecture, i.e. qualities of the business such as flexibility and efficiency, IT governance e.g. plan/organize and IT-systems for example availability and maintainability. By employing correlation analysis among these qualities we found that the companies prioritize these differently. Our main findings show that companies who prioritize performance also prioritize availability, that companies who prioritize interoperability also prioritize maintainability, that companies who prioritize usability also prioritize suitability, and that companies who prioritize decision support also prioritize control and follow up. Based on this correlation analysis future research focus can be concentrated on the most sought after aspects of EA. In the long run these aspects can influence the content of the EA metamodels used in different companies [10,8].

## 1.1   Outline

The remainder of this paper is structured as follows. Section 2 contrasts the present contribution with some related work in the fields of Enterprise Architecture. In section 3, the survey areas of IT-system qualities, business qualities and IT governance qualities are detailed, followed by a description of the data collection method in section 4. Section 5 is the locus of the main contribution, presenting the data collected through the survey along with an analysis. Section 6 contains a discussion of the results, and some concluding remarks are given in section 7.

## 2  Related Work

To place the present contribution in a proper context, this section outlines some related work and important concepts. The main research discipline is covered, namely enterprise architecture.

EA has been proposed as an approach for managing the business and IT on a strategic level. EA targets a holistic and unified scope of an organization [11,12]. This overarching perspective is also present in the ISO/IEC 42010:2007 standard, defining architecture as "the fundamental organization of a system, embodied in its components, their relationships to each other and the environment, and the principles governing its design and evolution" [13]. As a consequence of this wide scope, EA is typically not limited to IT, but also encompasses the relation and support of IT to the business. Thus, in many respects EA can be seen as a tool for achieving alignment between business and IT.

If the joint scope of IT and business is one defining part of EA, its model-based methodology is another. As the name hints, architectural descriptions are central in EA. These descriptions include entities covering a broad range of phenomena, such as strategic aspects, organizational structure, business processes, software and data, as well as IT infrastructure [2,3,14]. A large number of EA frameworks have been proposed by the community, each detailing the kind of entities that should be part of the modeling effort. Some examples are [4,15,16,17].

Essentially, EA models serve the purpose of helping various stakeholders in an organization to document and thus understand the complex enterprise, analyze the properties of current and potential future scenarios, plan and design future scenarios and the road to get there, as well as communicating the current and future state of affairs to other stakeholders in the organization. Furthermore, by focusing on particular needs of decision-makers – modeling not for modeling's sake, but for particular purposes – EA can be used as a powerful decision-support tool [6].

Wai Fong Boh and Daniel Yellin [18] present a study focusing on the employment of enterprise architecture standards and their effect on information technology management. They ask two research questions: (i) how do different governance mechanisms affect the use of EA standards? (ii) to what extent does the use of EA standards help organizations improve the sharing and integration of IT resources across the enterprise? These research questions are addressed by testing eight hypotheses, for instance: Organizations that have mechanisms to facilitate stakeholder involvement are more likely to see greater use of and conformance to EA standards. The hypotheses were tested with data collected in a survey sent to 47 organizations. 112 responses were obtained from the survey. By using the partial least squares (PLS)-based structural equation modeling (SEM) they found that (i) each type of governance mechanism had a different impact on each type of EA standard, and (ii) the use of EA standards was significant in helping organizations to effectively manage all four types of IT resources.

Sabine Buckl et al., in a survey of EA tools, investigate the expectations regarding EA amongst industrial practitioners [19]. However, the scope of this investigation differs from the scope of the present paper.

# 3    Research Framework

In the subsequent subsections, each of the three areas – (i) IT-system qualities, (ii) business qualities, and (iii) IT governance qualities – is detailed.

## 3.1    IT-System Qualities

The IT-system qualities employed are based on the ISO 9126 standard [13,20,21,22,23]. These qualities have also been used in the EA research at the Royal Institute of Technology (KTH), perhaps most prominently in the book "Enterprise Architecture – Models and analyses for information systems decision making" [6].

**Performance**, or efficiency, as the ISO/IEC 9126 labels it, is a quality that characterizes how much work a system can perform and how fast. Performance is defined as the degree to which an IT-system can meet its objective in terms of scalability and responsiveness [24].

**Interoperability** is described as the ability of two or more systems or components to exchange information and to use that information [25]. Interoperability is defined in terms of two kinds of data exchangeability, one related to data formats and the other related to a user's attempts to exchange data [13].

The **availability** of a system indicates how often a system is ready to deliver its services to its users. Post factum, availability is defined as the ratio between the system's time in service (uptime) and the total time (uptime plus downtime), [6,26].

The most common definition of IT-system **security** is how well the system is capable of preserving the confidentiality, integrity and availability of its internal information [27,28].

The **usability** of a system reflects how easy it is for a user to interact with and perform his or her tasks in the system. [21] defines usability as the understandability, learnability, operability and attractiveness of an IT-system.

The **accuracy** of an IT-system is measured by the degree to which it produces resulting data that is accurate and precise. This is determined by comparing the output value with the expected or "real" value [6].

The ease with which an IT-system can be modified or adapted to a changed environment is referred to as **maintainability**, sometimes also identified as modifiability [25]. Inspired by [29], maintainability is defined by five sub-qualities, viz. flexibility, reusability, extensibility, portability, and integrability. These describe the different kinds of changes a system can be exposed to during its lifetime.

The **suitability** of an IT-system is the degree to which the functionality of the system supports the system's intended work tasks. That is, a suitable system offers the functions specified in the requirements specification, and meets user expectations with regard to functionality. The definition of suitability used here is borrowed from [13]. This definition stipulates that a system's suitability is contingent upon the systems functional adequacy, functional implementation completeness, functional implementation coverage and functional specification stability.

## 3.2 Business Qualities

The business qualities are based on a taxonomy originally presented by [30], which is based on a literature consolidation of over 500 papers and 20 books. The particular subset of this taxonomy employed in the present survey is that used by [31].

**Flexibility** is defined as the degree to which the business processes and organizational units in a company have the ability to adapt to changes in market conditions/requirements, e.g. changed demand, political and economical factors.

**Efficiency** concerns the degree to which the business processes in a company exhibit short manufacturing times/lead times/cycle times/work times, much automation of work etc.

**Effectiveness** is the degree to which the business processes in a company produce what the market demands and spend little time on paperwork and administration.

**Integration and coordination** focuses on the degree to which the organizational units in a company have the ability to integrate and coordinate different parts of the organization, i.e. coordination of the production and the distribution department, of the sales and production planning departments etc.

**Decision support** deals with the degree to which an organizational unit has proper decision support, i.e. makes well-informed decisions, decisions are taken close to operations, decisions have high reliability and low uncertainty, decisions made are accepted by the organization etc.

**Control and follow up** is defined as the degree to which an organization have the ability to control and follow up work i.e. decisions are evaluated in retrospect, lessons learned are documented and re-used, new projects take previous experiences into account etc.

**Organizational culture** means to what degree the organizational culture in a company is appreciated by the people working at the company, i.e. there is a high job satisfaction and motivation, no negative stress, low numbers of sick leave etc.

## 3.3 IT Governance Qualities

The IT governance qualities are based on the four main processes of the well-known COBIT standard [32].

**Plan and organize** covers strategy and tactics, and concerns the identification of the way IT can best contribute to the achievement of the business objectives.

**Acquire and implement** is about realizing the IT strategy, identifying, developing, or acquiring IT solutions, as well as implementing and integrating these into the business processes.

**Deliver and support** is concerned with the actual delivery of required services, which includes service delivery, management of security and continuity, service support for users, and management of data and operational facilities.

**Monitor and evaluate** addresses performance management, monitoring of internal control, regulatory compliance and governance in order to keep or improve quality and compliance with control requirements.

Compared to the IT-system and business qualities, the IT governance qualities might prima facie look more like activities. However, this should be interpreted as an operationalization of IT governance qualities in terms of maturity of the IT processes. Thus, the IT processes per se are not our primary interest here.

# 4    Data Collection

An on-line survey was used for data collection. Prior to distribution, the survey was pretested to a select number of EA experts and valuable comments were received and addressed. Invitations were emailed to EA professionals in Sweden, Switzerland, Austria and Germany. The email addresses were condensed from the attendance lists of EA practitioner conferences that have been organized by the authoring institutions. Additionally a web link to the survey was posted on several EA community websites. Out of 1105 invitations sent, 92 emails bounced, 339 persons started and 174 persons completed the survey. The on-line survey was active for ten days (September 11-21, 2009). The survey included a final question regarding the respondent's confidence with his or her answers. Twelve persons stated weak confidence so their answers were not further considered. A total of 162 completely filled-out surveys are subjected to the analysis below. Figure 1 describes the dataset in detail.

The survey is comprised of four parts: Part one of the survey contains questions regarding the background of the respondents such as industry, country, and company size as well as the respondent's role and involvement with EA. Respondents employed by a consulting company had the option to answer on behalf of a client company. 43 respondents used this option. The second part of the survey has two sections. The first section contains questions addressing EA use for IT/business alignment and the importance and perceived maturity of

| Industry | Count | Percent |
|---|---|---|
| Financial industry | 49 | 30.2% |
| Utility | 23 | 14.2% |
| Manufacturing | 17 | 10.5% |
| Other | 13 | 8.0% |
| Transportation | 12 | 7.4% |
| Telecommunication | 10 | 6.2% |
| Software industry | 8 | 4.9% |
| Public sector | 7 | 4.3% |
| Defense/Military | 7 | 4.3% |
| IT/Management consulting | 4 | 2.5% |
| Health care/Pharmaceutical | 3 | 1.9% |
| Engineering/Architecture | 3 | 1.9% |
| Academia/Research | 2 | 1.2% |
| Tourism | 2 | 1.2% |
| Retail | 2 | 1.2% |
| | 162 | 100.0% |

| Size of company | Count | Percent |
|---|---|---|
| <100 employees | 15 | 9.3% |
| 100-1.000 | 32 | 19.8% |
| 1.001-5.000 | 33 | 20.4% |
| 5.001-10.000 | 15 | 9.3% |
| 10.001-25.000 | 28 | 17.3% |
| >25.000 | 39 | 24.1% |
| | 162 | 100.0% |

| Area of activity | Count | Percent |
|---|---|---|
| Business management | 28 | 17.3% |
| Business unit | 22 | 13.6% |
| IT department | 52 | 32.1% |
| IT management | 60 | 37.0% |
| | 162 | 100.0% |

| Country | Count | Percent |
|---|---|---|
| Austria | 4 | 2.5% |
| Finland | 1 | 0.6% |
| Germany | 28 | 17.3% |
| Sweden | 73 | 45.1% |
| Switzerland | 56 | 34.6% |
| | 162 | 100.0% |

**Fig. 1.** Data set description

IT/business alignment at the respondent's company. Section two contains more detailed questions related to IT/business alignment and the positioning of the IT department within the respondent's company. The third part of the survey addresses the qualities regarding IT, business, and IT governance as presented in section 3. For each quality one statement was posted and the respondents were asked to mark the actual (as-is) situation (degree of realization) and desired (to-be) situation (importance for future realization) on a five-point Likert scale (where 1 equals very low, 2 equals low, 3 equals medium, 4 equals high, and 5 equals very high). For the to-be situation, the respondents were cautioned to keep in mind that resources are limited and that the most important concerns need to be prioritized. The final part of the survey contains a question on the respondents' confidence regarding the answers, as well as the possibility to submit questions and feedback to the authors.

## 5    Analysis

The section aims at presenting the analysis of the data collected in the survey and the results obtained from this analysis. The first subsection presents descriptive data from the survey, while the second subsection presents an exploratory correlation analysis among the questions.

### 5.1    Enterprise Architecture – Descriptive Data

In the following, descriptive data from the survey is presented in the form of box plots. As is common, these plots contain five basic characteristics of the data sets: The maxima and minima, the median, and the first and third quartiles cutting off the lowest and the highest 25% of the data sets respectively. In addition, the plots also display the arithmetic means of the data sets (marked by asterisks, *).

Figure 2 displays experience of EA among the respondents. This is the only plot where outliers have been removed: one response on the tools question and two responses on each of the other questions claiming experience of more than 22 years have been removed. This cut-off limit was derived by setting the seminal Zachman 1987 publication [5] as a starting point for when it is meaningful to speak of EA and experience thereof.

As is evident from the plot, the adoption of models seems to precede the adoption of tools, processes and roles.

Figure 3 illustrates the perception of IT/business alignment among the respondents. It is clear that the respondents perceive that this issue is important in their companies, but not that the actual level of alignment is equally high. EA methods are perceived to support IT/business alignment to a moderate extent.

Figure 4 illustrates the perception of actual and desired situations with regard to software application and system concerns. One general trend that can be identified is that the future aspirations are higher than the present situation. The qualities are also valued slightly differently, with availability appearing as the most important concern and maintainability as the least important one.

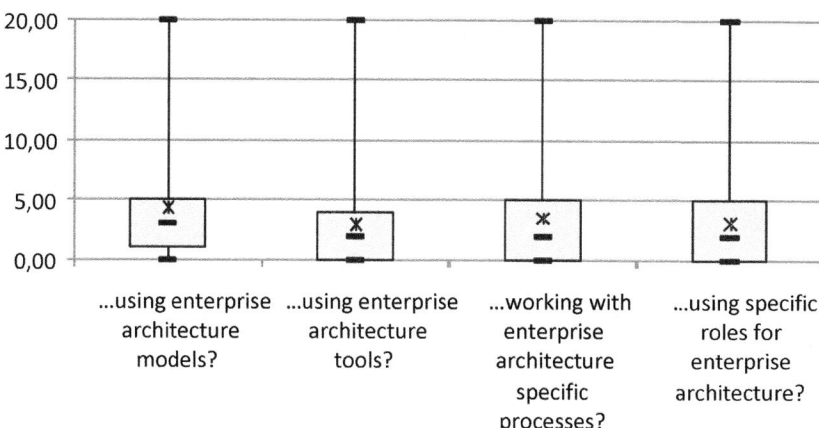

**Fig. 2.** Experience of EA among the respondents ($N = 160$, $N = 161$, $N = 160$, $N = 160$)

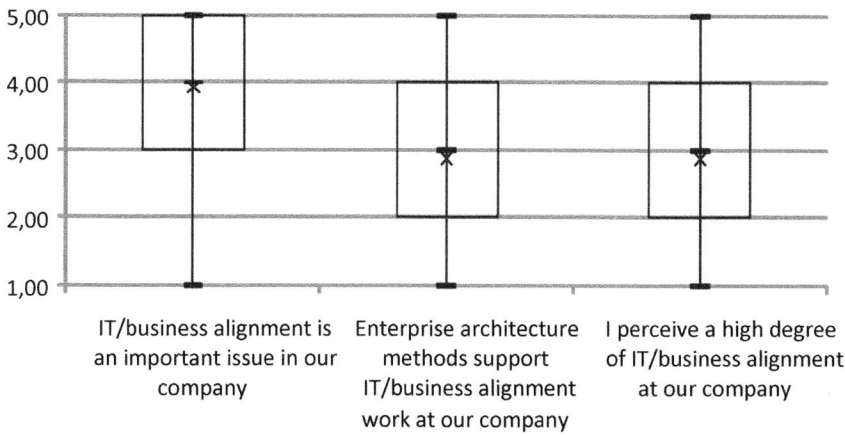

**Fig. 3.** The perception of IT/business alignment among the respondents ($N = 153$, $N = 159$, $N = 160$). Scale from 1 (very low) to 5 (very high).

Figure 5 illustrates the perception of actual and desired situations with regard to business concerns. Again, there is a trend of future aspirations that are higher than the present situation.

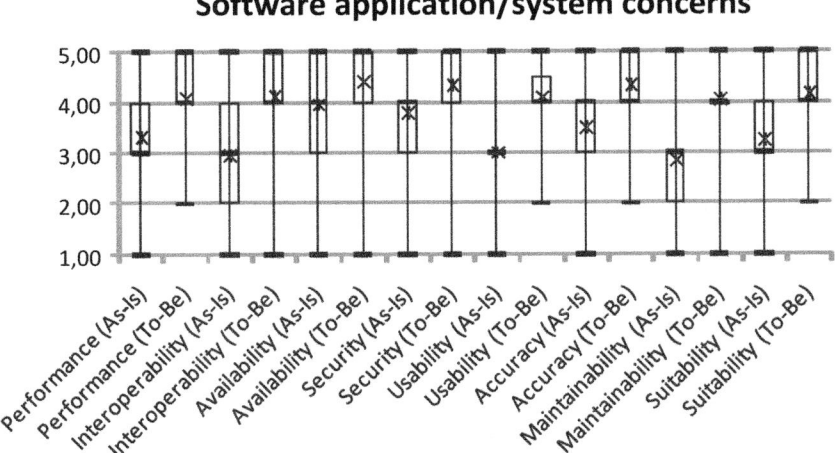

**Fig. 4.** The perception of actual and desired situations with regard to software application and system concerns ($N = 158$, $N = 158$, $N = 157$, $N = 158$, $N = 159$, $N = 158$, $N = 154$, $N = 157$, $N = 160$, $N = 159$, $N = 159$, $N = 156$, $N = 158$, $N = 155$, $N = 160$, $N = 160$). Scale from 1 (very low) to 5 (very high).

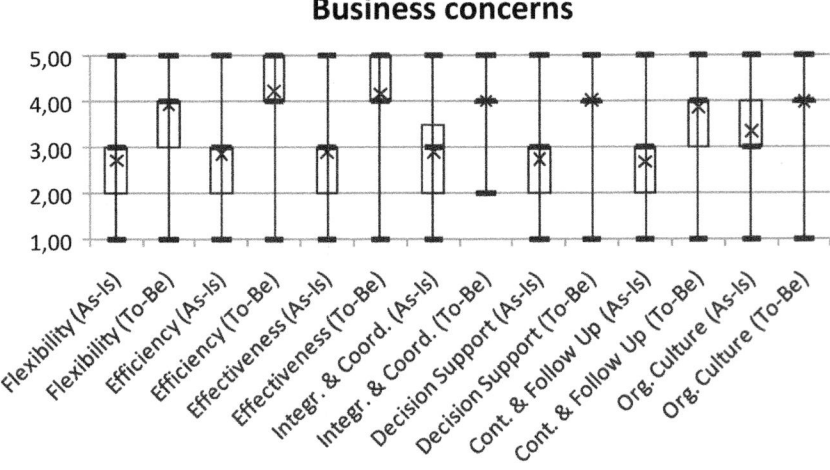

**Fig. 5.** The perception of actual and desired situations with regard to business concerns ($N = 160$, $N = 157$, $N = 159$, $N = 157$, $N = 158$, $N = 157$, $N = 159$, $N = 158$, $N = 158$, $N = 154$, $N = 160$, $N = 156$, $N = 156$, $N = 151$). Scale from 1 (very low) to 5 (very high).

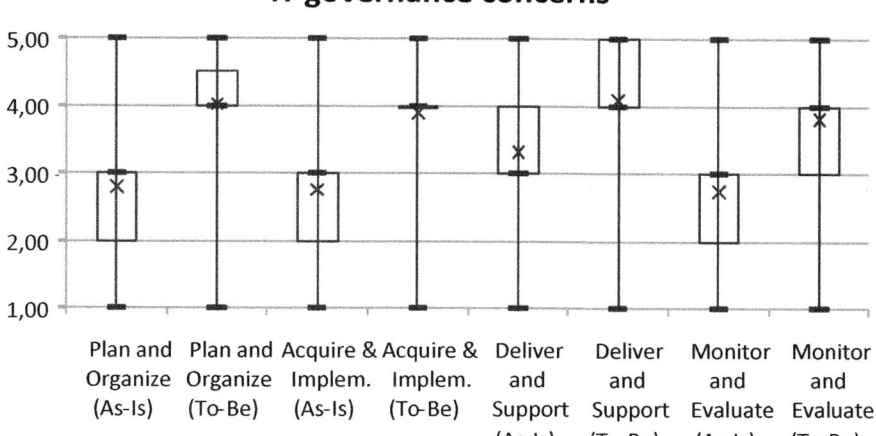

**Fig. 6.** The perception of actual and desired situations with regard to business concerns ($N = 160$, $N = 157$, $N = 159$, $N = 157$, $N = 158$, $N = 157$, $N = 159$, $N = 158$, $N = 158$, $N = 154$, $N = 160$, $N = 156$, $N = 156$, $N = 151$). Scale from 1 (very low) to 5 (very high).

Figure 6 illustrates the perception of actual and desired situations with regard to IT governance concerns. Again, the trend of future aspirations being higher than the present situation is apparent.

## 5.2   Qualities – Correlation and Descriptive Data

Secondly, the survey data was used for a more exploratory analysis of the correlations found in the survey material. By looking through the entire material for strong correlations ($> 0.5$) significant on the 0.01 level, a few interesting observations could be made:

The IT-systems quality attributes of *Performance* and *Availability* correlate strongly, both in the as-is situation (0.539) and the to-be situation (0.578), significant on the 0.01 level. This means that in companies where performance is an important concern, so is availability – and vice versa, that in companies where performance is not an important concern, neither is availability. This is a reasonable result, as these two qualities are rather similar. An IT-system that runs extremely slowly, i.e. shows poor performance, at some point simply should be considered completely unavailable.

The IT-systems quality attributes of *Interoperability* and *Maintainability* correlate strongly, both in the as-is situation (0.526) and the to-be situation (0.512), significant on the 0.01 level. This means that in companies where interoperability is an important concern, so is maintainability – and vice versa, that in companies where interoperability is not an important concern, neither is maintainability.

This is a reasonable result, as these two qualities often relate to each other. One important reason why IT-systems need to be maintained and modified throughout their life-cycle is to perform integrations with other systems, i.e. for interoperability purposes. Conversely, systems can be interoperable by virtue of being easy to maintain, viz. the changes needed to become interoperable can easily be brought about.

The IT-systems quality attributes of *Usability* and *Suitability* correlate strongly, both in the as-is situation (0.517) and the to-be situation (0.538), significant on the 0.01 level. This means that in companies where usability is an important concern, so is suitability – and vice versa, that in companies where usability is not an important concern, neither is suitability. This is a reasonable result, as it should be expected that an IT-system suitable for its task is more user-friendly than a less suitable one.

Turning to the business qualities, *Decision support* and *Control and follow up* correlate strongly, both in the as-is situation (0.565) and the to-be situation (0.538), significant on the 0.01 level. This means that in companies where decision support is an important concern, so is control and follow up – and vice versa, that in companies where decision support is not an important concern, neither is control and follow up. This is a reasonable result, since concern for good decision-making should make follow up of the decisions a priority as well.

In the area of business qualities, correlations between *Efficiency* and *Effectiveness* were also found. However, we are reluctant to make too much of these findings, as there is a considerable risk of semantic confusion being responsible for these correlations.

It should be noted that, apart from being significant on the 0.01 level, all the correlations described above hold for both the as-is situation and the to-be situation. In the authors' opinion, this makes them strong candidates for future investigations. Still, it should be emphasized that these correlations have been found by an explorative investigation, not by prior hypothesis. The results of this section are summarized in Table 1.

**Table 1.** Strong correlations ($> 0.5$) significant on the 0.01 level, between concerns for different qualities

| Quality 1 | Quality 2 | As-is correlation | To-be correlation |
|---|---|---|---|
| Performance | Availability | 0.539 | 0.578 |
| Interoperability | Maintainability | 0.526 | 0.512 |
| Usability | Suitability | 0.517 | 0.538 |
| Decision support | Control and follow up | 0.565 | 0.538 |

## 6   Discussion

Considering the results presented in section 5, it is striking how some simple patterns re-appear throughout the survey results:

1. The differences between as-is qualities within each of the IT-system, business and IT governance categories are not very large. It seems that the bulk of companies judge themselves to be somewhere in the middle with regard to most IT-system, business and IT governance qualities.
2. The differences between to-be qualities are similarly small. This is more interesting, since the survey explicitly asked for *prioritizations* when it comes to the to-be situation. With limited resources, all qualities cannot be prioritized. The fact that the to-be responses, over the board, looks like just slightly elevated versions of the as-is responses is disconcerting. Three explanations are possible:
   (i) The respondents themselves have tried to prioritize, but failed.
   (ii) The respondents have truthfully reported the situation at their companies, and it is the companies that have failed to prioritize.
   (iii) The answers are due to the structure and formulation of the survey.

   Explanation (iii) is certainly the case to some extent. For example, the on-line survey could have been programmed to force rankings from the respondents, rather than merely asking for them. Nevertheless, explanations (i) and (ii) are probably also present, indicating a lack of ability or willingness to prioritize on the part of either (i) individual respondents or (ii) their companies.

The explorative search for strong correlations reveals a few interesting pairs of concerns, as summarized in Table 1. A potential implication is that research dealing with these qualities could be made more useful by also taking the correlated quality into account. Thus, interoperability research such as [33] could be deemed more relevant by practitioners if also taking maintainability research such as [34] into account, and vice versa.

## 7   Conclusions

There is a disconcerting trend to be found in the survey responses, viz. the inability to prioritize. While this trend ought to be further investigated – using methods that eliminate the risk of spurious answers – some preliminary conclusions can be drawn.

An implication for the communities of research, consultancy, tool vending etc. is the need to help companies prioritize properly. Note that this implication holds even if this survey trend is a spurious result of the way the questions were asked – if so, this shows how vulnerable the ability to prioritize is to haphazard circumstances.

If Enterprise Architecture is to become successful, it must not fall victim to company inability to prioritize, followed by thin-spread resources, and resulting disappointments. Interesting future work thus naturally includes research into the impact of prioritization – to what extent does the success of Enterprise Architecture depend on proper prioritization? Another area of future work is further investigation of the strong correlations found between concerns for various IT-system, business and IT governance qualities.

One additional implication for the research community is due to the pairs of concerns, as summarized in Table 1. This pairing can be used to make research on one concern more relevant by also including aspects of the other concern.

# References

1. Ross, J.W., Weill, P., Robertson, D.: Enterprise Architecture As Strategy: Creating a Foundation for Business Execution. Harvard Business School Press, Boston (August 2006)
2. Lankhorst, M.: Enterprise Architecture At Work. Springer, Heidelberg (2005)
3. Winter, R., Fischer, R.: Essential layers, artifacts, and dependencies of enterprise architecture. Journal of Enterprise Architecture 3(2), 7–18 (2007)
4. The Open Group: The Open Group Architecture Framework (TOGAF) - version 9. The Open Group (2009)
5. Zachman, J.A.: A framework for information systems architecture. IBM Syst. J. 26(3), 276–292 (1987)
6. Johnson, P., Ekstedt, M.: Enterprise Architecture – Models and Analyses for Information Systems Decision Making. Studentlitteratur (2007)
7. Kurpjuweit, S., Winter, R.: Viewpoint-based meta model engineering. In: Enterprise Modelling and Information Systems Architectures, EMISA (2007)
8. Saat, J., Franke, U., Lagerström, R., Ekstedt, M.: Enterprise architecture meta models for IT/business alignment situations. In: Proc. 14th IEEE International EDOC Conference, EDOC 2010 (to appear, October 2010)
9. Saat, J., Winter, R., Franke, U., Lagerström, R., Ekstedt, M.: Analysis of IT/business alignment situations as a precondition for the design and engineering of situated IT/business alignment solutions. In: Proc. Hawaii International Conference on System Sciences (HICSS-44) (to appear, January 2011)
10. Lagerström, R., Saat, J., Franke, U., Aier, S., Ekstedt, M.: Enterprise meta modeling methods - combining a stakeholder-oriented and a causality-based approach. In: Enterprise, Business-Process and Information Systems Modeling. LNBIP, vol. 29, pp. 381–393. Springer, Heidelberg (June 2009) ISSN 1865-1348
11. Rohloff, M.: Framework and Reference for Architecture Design. In: Proceedings of the 14th Americas Conference on Information Systems (AMCIS 2008), Toronto, pp. 1–14 (2008)
12. Tyler, D., Cathcart, T.: A structured method for developing agile enterprise architectures. In: Proceedings of the International Conference on Agile Manufacturing (ICAM 2006), Norfolk, Virginia, USA, pp. 1–8 (2006)
13. International Standardization Organization/International Electrotechnical Committee: ISO/IEC 42010:2007 - Systems and software engineering – Recommended practice for architectural description of software-intensive systems. Technical report, ISO (2007)
14. Jonkers, H., Lankhorst, M., ter Doest, H., Arbab, F., Bosma, H., Wieringa, R.: Enterprise architecture: Management tool and blueprint for the organisation. Information Systems Frontiers 8(2), 63–66 (2006)
15. Department of Defense Architecture Framework Working Group: DoD Architecture Framework, version 1.5. Technical report, Department of Defense, USA (2007)
16. Lankhorst, M., Proper, H., Jonkers, H.: The Architecture of the ArchiMate Language. In: Halpin, T., et al. (eds.) BPMDS 2009 and EMMSAD 2009. LNBIP, vol. 29, pp. 367–380. Springer, Heidelberg (2009)

17. Ministry of Defence: MOD Architecture Framework version 1.2.003. Technical report, Ministry of Defence, UK (September 2008)
18. Boh, W., Yellin, D.: Using enterprise architecture standards in managing information technology. Journal of Management Information Systems 23(3), 163–207 (2007)
19. Buckl, S., Dierl, T., Matthes, F., Ramacher, R., Schweda, C.: Current and future tool support for ea management. In: Proceedings of Workshop MDD, SOA und IT-Management (MSI 2008), Oldenburg, Gito. (2008)
20. International Organization for Standardization: Software engineering–product quality–part 2: External metrics. International standard ISO/IEC TR 9126–2:2003(E), International Organization for Standardization (July 2003)
21. International Organization for Standardization: Software engineering–product quality–part 1: Quality model. International standard ISO/IEC TR 9126–1:2001(E), International Organization for Standardization (June 2001)
22. International Organization for Standardization: Software engineering–product quality–part 3: Internal metrics. International standard ISO/IEC TR 9126–3:2003(E), International Organization for Standardization (July 2003)
23. International Organization for Standardization: Software engineering–product quality–part 4: Quality in use metrics. International standard ISO/IEC TR 9126–4:2004(E), International Organization for Standardization (April 2004)
24. Smith, C., Williams, L.: Performance Solutions: a practical guide to creating responsive, scalable software. Addison-Wesley, Boston (2002)
25. IEEE Standards Board: IEEE Standard Glossary of Software Engineering Technology. Technical report, The Institute of Electrical and Electronics Engineers (September 1990)
26. Franke, U., Johnson, P., König, J., Marcks von Würtemberg, L.: Availability of enterprise IT systems – an expert-based Bayesian model. In: Proc. Fourth International Workshop on Software Quality and Maintainability (WSQM 2010), Madrid (March 2010)
27. Ferraiolo, D., Kuhn, D., Chandramouli, R.: Role-based access control. Artech House Publishers, Norwood (2003)
28. Dhillon, G., Backhouse, J.: Technical opinion: Information system security management in the new millennium. Communications of the ACM 43(7), 128 (2000)
29. Matinlassi, M., Niemelä, E.: The impact of maintainability on component-based software systems. In: Proceedings of the 29th IEEE EUROMICRO Conference "New Waves in System Architecture" (2003)
30. Gammelgård, M., Ekstedt, M., Gustafsson, P.: A categorization of benefits from IS/IT investments. In: Eurpoean Conference on Information Technology Evaluation (September 2006)
31. Gustafsson, P., Franke, U., Höök, D., Johnson, P.: Quantifying IT impacts on organizational structure and business value with extended influence diagrams, vol. 15, pp. 138–152. Springer, Heidelberg (November 2008)
32. The IT Governance Institute: Control Objectives for Information and Related Technology (COBIT) 4.1. Technical report, The IT Governance Institute (2007)
33. Ullberg, J., Lagerström, R., Ekstedt, M.: A framework for interoperability analysis on the semantic web using architecture models. In: Proceedings of Workshop on Enterprise Interoperability (IWEI 2008) (September 2008)
34. Lagerström, R., Johnson, P., Höök, D.: Architecture analysis of enterprise systems modifiability – models, analysis and validation. The Journal of Systems and Software 83, 1387–1403 (to appear, 2010)

# An Enterprise-Wide Intervention at IRS: A Longitudinal Analysis of Stakeholder Sentiments

Sandeep Purao[1] and Kevin Desouza[2]

[1] College of Information Sciences & Technology The Pennsylvania State University,
University Park State College, PA 16802
spurao@ist.psu.edu
[2] Information School, University of Washington, Seattle, WA 98101
Kev.desouza@gmail.com

**Abstract.** The Internal Revenue Service Business Modernization Project undertaken by the Tax Agency of the US Government has been singled out as an example of a massive failure. As envisioned, the project was intended as an Enterprise-wide intervention that would provide modern services and effective data access to citizenry and several government agencies. After more than a decade and 3 billion dollars later, the results appear to be less than exemplary. This paper identifies different stakeholders who participated in the project, and analyzes the sentiments and confidence each expressed with a view to understanding what and how things may or may not have worked. We conclude with lessons learned from our investigation including recognizing the importance of multiple stakeholders for Enterprise-wide initiatives.

## 1 Introduction

Enterprise architecture represents the planning for and explicit arrangement of several components of an enterprise to ensure that the enterprise goals are met in an effective and efficient manner. It addresses not only the underlying business logic but also the information technology infrastructure that is designed to support the business logic. Enterprise-wide initiatives to understand, refine, and sometimes drastically overhaul this architecture are, therefore, a necessary component of realizing the vision of a more effective and efficient enterprise architecture. These initiatives can take many forms including organizational change, application portfolio management as well as enterprise-wide initiatives to radically transform both the technology infrastructure as well as business practice.

The IRS modernization project (Phillips 2009) was an example of the third strategy: a radical transformation of both the information technology infrastructure as well as the business practices. Given its sub-par performance, it was also a project that was reviled by practitioners and consultants alike (see, e.g. Charrette 2005). In this paper, we consider this project as an example of an Enterprise-wide Initiative aimed at Architectural Re-organization. The involvement of a wide range of stakeholders, both internal and external, is a pre-requisite for such efforts.

These stakeholders may each have a different agenda, and may, as a result, perceive the re-organization and re-architecting effort differently. Their perceptions of the project will

E. Proper et al. (Eds.): TEAR 2010, LNBIP 70, pp. 30–43, 2010.

not only determine how they participate in the effort but will also be a significant contributor to determining overall project progress. In a sense, the stakeholders may act as distributed sensors as well as signal activators through the project. With hindsight, one can make sense of why certain attitudes changed and based on these, speculate about possible clues that may be seen as early indicators of how the re-architecting effort is progressing. This research was, therefore, undertaken with in an open-ended research question.

•       What can longitudinal analyses of stakeholder sentiments and expressed confidence reveal about the progress of a re-architecting effort?

As we continue this project, we hope to discover early clues to project success or predict impending project failures. The analysis may allow us to identify clusters of stakeholders, and identify internal as well as external sources of project risk. And it may provide an understanding of how the network of stakeholders may evolve through the effort. The techniques we report in this paper represent analyses for the first step of the project. They include Sentiment and Confidence analysis following content analysis techniques (see Weber 1996 for a recent introduction), extended and refined for the purpose of this research. With these techniques, we analyze publicly available documents such as assessment documents and press reports to map the sentiments expressed by different stakeholders over time. The key contribution of this research is the explication of several longitudinal analyses of stakeholder sentiments and associated interpretations, which may reveal problems and concerns about the project as well as the evolution of the network of stakeholders.

## 2   Prior Work

### 2.1   Large Scale Enterprise (Re-)Architecting Efforts

Much writing about Enterprise Architecture (EA) implicates multiple layers and inter-dependencies among these. A number of definitions, for example, assert that the definition of a "system" from IEEE Standard 610.12 or UML 1.3 may provide a useful starting point to understand EA efforts. The definition includes: a collection of connected units that are organized to accomplish a specific purpose, or a collection of components organized to accomplish a specific function or set of functions. The Architecture of a System is then defined, again following ANSI/IEEE Standard 1471-2000 as: the fundamental organization of a system, embodied in its components, their relationships to each other and the environment, and the principles governing its design and evolution. A similar idea is expounded by TOGAF, emphasizing the formal description as well as the structure of the components of a system. TOGAF, however, expands the definition to include the principles and guidelines governing the design and evolution of the components within the system over time.

This, more dynamic, viewpoint is also encapsulated by the Clinger-Cohen Act, which focuses on the IT Architecture: "The term `information technology architecture', with respect to an executive agency, means an integrated framework for evolving or maintaining existing information technology and acquiring new information technology to achieve the agency's strategic goals and information resources management goals." With additional such definitions, the separation and inter-dependencies among the different levels is also emphasized, such as The Open Group's definition, which includes: business architecture (business strategy, governance, organization, and key processes), data/information architecture (structure of an organization's logical and physical data resources), application architecture (a blueprint for the individual application systems to be deployed, their interactions, and their relationships to the core processes), and information technology architecture (software infrastructure intended to support the deployment of core, mission-critical applications). This multi-layer and complex view of architecture is also compared to the view of Enterprise Architecture as "system of systems" (Brownsword et al. 2006).

A dynamic view of Enterprise Architecture, then, is sometimes described as "Architecting" instead of "Architecture" (a verb instead of a noun). The multiple layers and inter-dependencies across these layers means Enterprise Architecting is, of necessity, a large and complex endeavor that can take a long time and consume significant organizational resources. By its very definition, a Re-Architecting process can change the relationships among stakeholders and may change the population of stakeholders as well. Large-scale re-architecting efforts are, therefore, comparable to large scale interventions in a system of systems, where the intervention can change the balance of power among stakeholders, adjust reward systems and reposition alliances, all either as a result of or in conjunction with changes to the underlying application, data and technology infrastructure. The case we study in this paper is one such example of re-architecting, brought about by external forces, which resulted in significant changes in the different architectural components.

### 2.2 Stakeholder Analysis in Project Management

Viewing the re-architecting effort as a large-scale project requires us to consider the different stakeholders that may be part of the effort. This perspective is useful because it allows a time-bound view of the re-architecting effort and allows us to use prior research related to project management (e.g. Aaltonen 2010). A particular stream of work from this domain that is useful to us is the idea of multiple stakeholders and how these stakeholder relationships can be managed. Much prior research suggests that stakeholder analysis must be an active component for successful project management. This includes activities such as stakeholder identification, stakeholder recruitment and stakeholder negotiations. Each is intended to increase the likelihood of success in large projects, which are invariably linked to changes in availability of information and other resources and consequent changes in the balance of power (Markus and Robey 1988). In addition, the work also suggests that stakeholder analysis for large-scale re-architecting efforts should include not only internal stakeholders but also external stakeholders. For the case we study in this paper, this notion of internal as well as external stakeholders operationalized as citizenry as well other government agencies is particularly important.

## 3  The Case: The IRS Business Systems Modernization Effort

### 3.1  Context

The Business Systems Modernization (BSM) program was threatened ever since its inception (in 1999) by delays, scope reductions, funding reductions, and poor costing

(Gardiner 2002; Gardiner 2003; Gardiner 2004; George 2005; George 2006; George 2007; George 2008; George 2009; Williams, 1999; Williams; 2000; Williams, 2002). As late as 2007, that is, after eight years of efforts, several systems considered a part of the BSM program were still incomplete and behind schedule (Phillips 2007). A module illustrative of the problems that IRS faced is the Customer Account Data Engine (referred to as CADE). This module, designed to process and store income tax returns, was supposed to be the 'centerpiece throughout the life of the Modernization Program' (Phillips, 2009). However, after a decade of implementation efforts (that is, as of 2009), only 30% of individual income tax returns were processed through this module (Phillips 2009). Contrast this with what the IRS had originally projected: that this module would be completed by 2005. Instead, in 2007, the IRS changed its estimated completion date for this module to 2012 (George 2006); and in 2009, the IRS suspended development of the module (White 2009).

The BSM project was conceived in response to the bill, signed into law by then President Clinton on July 22, 1998. The Internal Revenue Service (IRS) Restructuring Reform Act of 1998 (RRA 98) required the IRS, among other things, to restructure itself to better serve taxpayers and mandated that the IRS improve its systems for this purpose (Watts, Groen, Matsubara, Hovey & Whittle 2005). The program was considered inherently important to IRS because of its close association to the IRS's stated mission: "provide America's taxpayers top quality service by helping them understand and meet their tax responsibilities and by applying the tax law with integrity and fairness to all" (Internal Revenue Service 2007). The mandate for systems modernization lead to the first contract that the IRS entered into with Computer Sciences Corporation (CSC). CSC was charged with assembling a team of contractors, known as the PRIME Alliance, to develop new systems for the IRS to achieve modernization (Williams 1999; Internal Revenue Service 1998). The IRS also created a Business Systems Modernization (BSM) Office that was charged with leading the IRS's acquisition and implementation of new technology (Williams 1999). By 2009, the cumulative amount of funding spent on the BSM program is nearing USD 3 billion (Phillips 2009). In addition to the problems with the CADE module , a number of other challenges continue to plague the effort (see Table 1).

**Table 1.** BSM Program: Key Challenges (TIGTA 2009)

| |
|---|
| • Development of long-term systems requirements challenging. |
| • Continued weaknesses in program and contract management. |
| • Problems identified with security controls. |
| • IRS acknowledges that a "strategy correction" is needed. |
| • Difficulties in obtaining qualified personnel and sufficient funding. |

### 3.2 Stakeholders

As a complex and large-scale Enterprise Re-architecting effort, the BSM project involved several external stakeholders (see Table 2).

**Table 2.** External Stakeholders in the IRS BSM Project

- The Treasury Department
- The US Congress
- The General Accounting Office (GAO)
- Contractor
- Taxpayers

The Treasury Department is responsible for overseeing the IRS, including but not limited to managing federal finances, supervising national banks, designing currency, and advising on economic policy (U.S. Department of the Treasury 2008). The Restructuring Reform Act (RRA 98) required the Treasury Department to create two roles, which have published frequent reports about the BSM program. These roles include: (a) a Treasury Inspector General for Tax Administration (TIGTA), reporting to the Treasury Secretary, to conduct audits, investigations, and evaluation of IRS programs and operations (Watts et al., 2005); and (b) an IRS Oversight Board, consisting of nine members – six who are neither federal officers nor federal employees, one full-time federal employee, the Treasury Secretary (or Deputy Secretary if responsibility delegated), and the IRS Commissioner (Watts et al. 2005) – to review strategic plans and operational functions of the IRS (Watts et al. 2005).

The US Congress is responsible for passing tax laws that taxpayers are required to comply with. The IRS is responsible for incorporating new tax laws into its systems, communications, and procedures in time for taxpayers to comply with these new laws. After receiving a proposed budget from the US President's office each year, the US Congress is also responsible for approving the level of funding for federal programs, including the IRS BSM program.

The General Accounting Office (GAO) is responsible for monitoring the progress and performance of BSM and report on it because the US Congress has deemed it sufficiently important. The GAO describes itself as, "the U.S. Government Accountability Office (GAO) is an independent, nonpartisan agency that works for Congress. Often called the 'congressional watchdog,' GAO investigates how the federal government spends taxpayer dollars" (U.S. Government Accountability Office 2010). Similar to the TIGTA and the IRS Oversight Board, the GAO has published frequent reports addressing the BSM program, at the request of the US Congress.

Contractors are external IT vendors and staff to whom the IRS outsources systems work. Computer Sciences Corporation (CSC) was contracted by the IRS to lead the PRIME Alliance. In the early stages of the BSM program, CSC was responsible for hiring other contractors and coordinating their work (Gardiner 2005). However, in early 2005, the IRS scaled back the role of CSC and took on the role of system integrator, leaving CSC largely in a systems development role (Gardiner 2005). In addition to CSC, several others have been involved with the BSM program in different capacities.

Taxpayers are one of the primary users of many BSM systems. TIGTA reports reflect that the IRS typically defines BSM program goals, at least partly, in terms of taxpayer benefits (Gardiner 2002; Gardiner 2003; Gardiner 2004; George 2005;

George 2006; George 2007; George 2008; George 2009; Williams, 1999; Williams 2000; Williams 2002). They also indirectly fund the BSM effort with taxes paid.

There were several *internal stakeholders* as well (see Table 3).

**Table 3.** Internal Stakeholders in the IRS BSM Project

| |
|---|
| • Senior Management |
| • Taxpayer Divisions |
| • The Internal IT Organization |
| • Contractor |
| • Taxpayers |

Senior Management is made up of the IRS Commissioner who has the most senior position within the IRS. During the BSM project, three separate individuals have held this office. In addition, the senior management is made up of the CIO (and since 2998, the role of a CTO).

Taxpayer Divisions were created in October 2000 in response to the RRA 98 mandate, which required the IRS to reorganize so that it could better serve taxpayers (Williams 2000). The Divisions serve specific taxpayer segments (Williams 2000) such as Wage and Investment earners, Self Employed individuals, or non-profits, among others (IRS 2009). They represent important stakeholders for the BSM program because they are highly involved in defining business requirements.

The Internal IT organization includes several divisions such as the Information Systems organization, the Business Systems Modernization Office, the Modernization and Information Technology Services organization, which includes Applications Development, Enterprise Services, a Program Integration Office and a Program Management Office were added (Phillips 2009).

Additional stakeholders, excluding IT organizations, within the IRS included the following functions (IRS 2009): Criminal Investigation, Office of Professional Responsibility, Whistleblower Office, Agency-Wide Shared Services, Human Capital, Finance, and the Office of Privacy, Information Protection and Data Security.

Given the scale and complexity of the project and the number of stakeholders involved, our efforts in this research were aimed at understanding how the different stakeholders perceived the BSM program, and their attitudes towards the program. The next section outlines the methodology followed to uncover these.

## 4 Research Approach and Application

### 4.1 Research Approach

The methodology followed for this research combined automated sentiment analysis (Gregory et al. 2009) with case study (Yin 2003). The sentiment analysis was made possible by a historical analysis of documents (such as press releases, audit reports and the like) created by stakeholders in the BSM program. As in other automated sentiment analysis studies and studies focusing on analysis of historical documents (Umapathy et al. 2009), we acknowledge that these documents may not reveal the stakeholders' personal agendas, the full nature of inter-personal communication, compromises incentives or secret caucus results. Others who study historical organizational processes express similar caveats (see, e.g. Langley 1999). Nevertheless, these documents reveal essential characteristics that allow inferences about project progress. The documents analyzed in the study came from the following sources: TIGTA, GAO, CSC, Government Computer News, Accounting Web, GovExec, IRS Press Releases, and Washington Technology.

These, publicly available documents, describe how the different stakeholders reflected on project progress and their own role in the re-architecting effort. The specific technique we used to analyze the documents was Sentiment and Confidence Analysis (see Weber 1996). Sentiment analysis is a methodology that computes the strength of sentiment expressed in a document by analyzing the content in the document. A number of specific techniques have been proposed for sentiment analysis (see, e.g. Gregory et al. 2009). Prior work shows that although sophisticated techniques such as parsing phrases and sentences, analyzing segments such as paragraphs, and identifying parts of compound sentences are available; the incremental gains tend to be not very large.

For the purpose of post-fact historical analysis, and analyzing trends, minimal techniques are, therefore, appropriate and adequate. We, therefore, followed the list of tags from the General Inquirer set of tags and enhanced for the purpose of this analysis. These tags are commonly used words in English that, if present in a document, likely indicate the tone of the document. For example, the presence of words (such as 'Improve' or 'Challenge') may suggest that the tone of the document is positive or negative, respectively. Similarly, another set of words (such as 'Approximately' or 'Significant'), if present in a document, likely indicate that the language in the document is understated or overstated, respectively. The set of words is accessible from http://www.wjh.harvard.edu/~inquirer/homecat.htm. Our enhancements to the list of words came mainly in the form of discarding certain words. For example, the word 'Tax' was considered a negative keyword in the original set. However, its occurrence in the BSM documents was not tied to this meaning. It was, therefore, removed. Other examples included the word 'Oversight,' because of the IRS Oversight Board as a stakeholder; the word 'Return,' which was removed as a positive keyword because of its connotation as a tax return; the word 'Prime,' which was removed as a positive keyword because it referred to the Prime contractor for the BSM program.

Based on the enhanced set of words, two measures were devised. The first, Confidence, computed the relative Confidence (Overstated vs. Understated words) in each document. A corresponding measure was developed to compute relative Sentiment (Positive vs. Negative words) in each document. In both cases, in spite of the possibility of some loss of data, the net occurrence of Overstated versus Understated or Positive versus Negative words was computed. For example, a document containing 15 occurrences of Positive words and 3 occurrences of Negative words would yield a numerator of 12; the total number of tokens in the document would yield the denominator (e.g. 300); and the measure would be computed as a fraction, in this case, 4%. The measures are shown below.

Confidence =  (# Net Tokens that are Overstated) / (# Tokens)
Sentiment =   (# Net Tokens that are Positive) / (# Tokens)

The intended analysis for each document was, therefore, meant to produce a placement for each document in a two-dimensional space along the two dimensions of Confidence and Sentiment. For example, we might expect that a Report from the Prime Contractor may appear as Positive Understated if the Prime Contractor follows the strategy of promising low and delivering high. On the other hand, an audit report may be cautious and may highlight negatives, suggesting a placement in the Negative Overstated quadrant. Over time, the placement of each document in the quadrants would then reveal the trajectory of progress and seeing the trajectory from the perspective of different stakeholders would allow an analysis of how each saw its own participation in the project and assessed project progress. A corpus of text was constructed based on the documents. For each document, the text tokens were extracted using simple text processing mechanisms. The set of tokens produced for each document was then used to compute the above measures.

## 5  Results

The results are described next with the help of Longitudinal Confidence and Sentiment analyses for three key stakeholders. We have elected to highlight these stakeholders because they represent core participants in the BSM re-architecting effort. Before describing how perceptions of these individual stakeholders evolved, it is useful to provide a broader characterization of project progress. We provide this as a set of qualitative comments based on the data analysis.

First, the aggregate data analysis following a longitudinal lens (*not shown here*) suggested a distinct downward trend in the sentiments expressed by the stakeholders. It showed that the first negative marker appeared in 2000, the year after the BSM project was started. In 2001 and 2002, the sentiment turned further negative marked by data points that showed a negative sentiment of 3% although balanced by two significantly positive statements. The general sentiment recovered in 2003 and 2004 only to sink again significantly in 2005 and 2006 with two negative data points in 2005 and one that was significantly negative at 5% in 2006. From 2007 onwards, although the sentiment was not negative, it did not provide a positive endorsement.

Second, the overall data analysis (*not shown here*) suggested a preponderance of reports from the Government Computer News that were Positive and Overstated. However, it is only reports from the same source that also appeared in the other three quadrants: Positive and Understated, Negative and Overstated, and Negative and Understated. In contrast, the few reports from the Prime Contractor all appeared as Positive as well as Overstated. A comparison with reports from the Government Accountability Office points to the almost uniform toning down of Positive sentiment. The press releases from IRS also appear as Positive and Overstated but less so compared to those by the Prime Contractor. The analysis suggests that there are clear differences across stakeholder groups. These analyses provided the backdrop for longitudinal analyses of individual stakeholders, shown next. Figure 1 shows a longitudinal view of Sentiment and Confidence in the documents prepared by TIGTA.

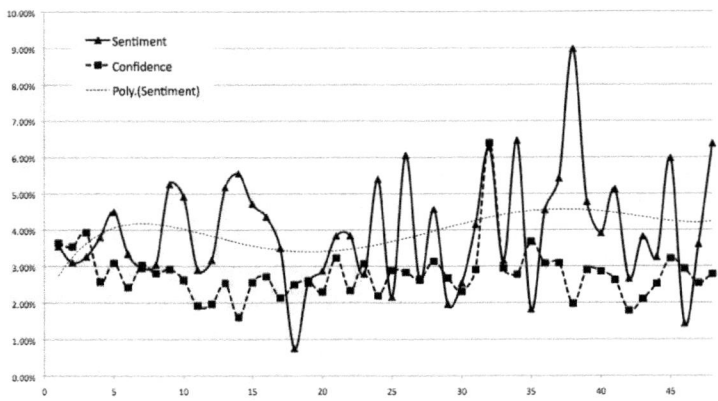

**Fig. 1.** Longitudinal Sentiment and Confidence Analysis for TIGTA

The data suggests some interesting interpretations. First, it points to *increasing volatility in Sentiment* over time (solid line). From early, more steady perceptions of the project, the TIGTA documents an indication of increased volatility. Two data points (significant Negative sentiment and significant Positive sentiment) occur when the zig-zag is violated. The polynomial trendline for Sentiment analysis (dotted line) also suggests this volatility dampening over time. Second, the data also points to a *slightly downward trend for Confidence* over time (dashed line). Although a trendline is not shown in the figure, a visual inspection confirms this trend. Together, the increased volatility in sentiment and downward confidence levels suggests that TIGTA is striving to portray a realistic picture of the BSM re-architecting effort. The next figure shows comparable measures based on documents produced by the GAO.

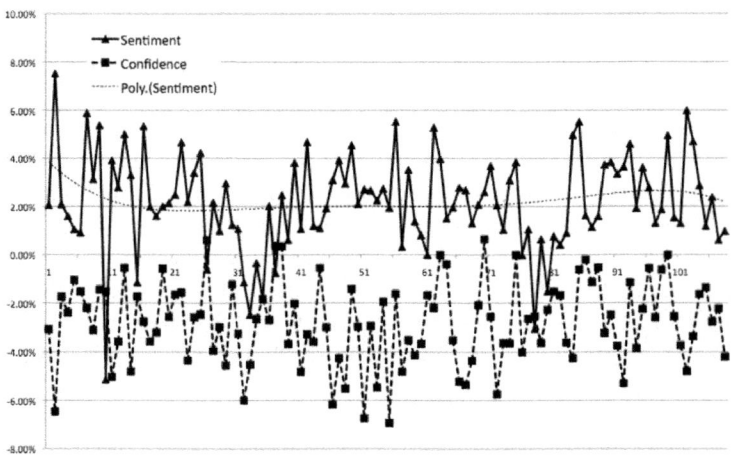

**Fig. 2.** Longitudinal Sentiment and Confidence Analysis for GAO

The longitudinal data from GAO documents suggests a *lowering of volatility and slightly downward trend for Sentiment* (see solid line for data and dotted line for trend in Figure 2). The longer-term *trend appears to be stable for Confidence*. Together, the GAO provides a consistent assessment that recognizes the troubled nature of the BSM effort. Comparing these with TIGTA documents, the high point for Sentiment analysis appears early for GAO (compared to that for TIGTA). The low point for Confidence also appears early for GAO (compared to that for TIGTA). The differences between TIGTA and GAO can be explained by their respective roles. TIGTA is a potential user and beneficiary of the system. As a result, TIGTA may be more aware of the complexity of the situation. The assessment of higher negative as well as higher positive sentiment later in the project progress may reflect what TIGTA has learned over time via its participation. In contrast, the GAO, without the benefit of an operational perspective, may be more swayed by promises for higher efficiencies and payoffs, contributing to higher positive sentiment accompanied by a lower confidence (reflecting its watchdog profile). With greater evidence, it may be able to arrive at a more balanced portrayal of the effort. The data points for the analysis of confidence for GAO are also significantly lower in absolute terms than that for TIGTA indicative of the watchdog profile it must fulfill. A comparison of theses two stakeholders, therefore, reveals that the Beneficiary vs. Monitor roles can produce different impressions about project progress. A third perspective we analyze is that from the Prime Contractor, CSC, as shown in figure 3 below.

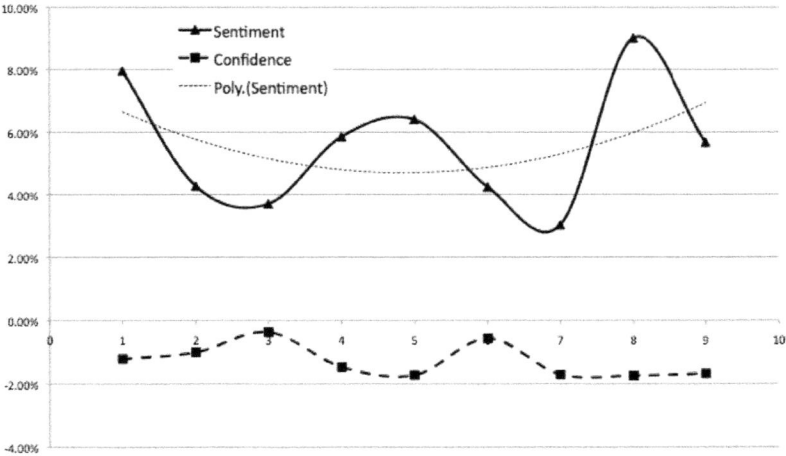

**Fig. 3.** Longitudinal Sentiment and Confidence Analysis for CSC

The data for CSC (although based on fewer documents) is noteworthy for displaying the *most even keel for confidence levels among the three stakeholders* analyzed so far. As the figures show, TIGTA is consistently in the plus territory, CSC never dips below minus two, whereas GAO routinely reaches minus five (see dotted lines in Figures 1-3). This perspective from CSC is interesting, for example, it may be seen as a policy of underpromising and overperforming. On the other hand, the sentiment analysis resembles what has been described as a bathtub-effect in software engineering efforts, where early enthusiasm gives way to realization of problems of scale and complexity, ending with a renewed sense of accomplishment with achievement of goals (see dotted trendline for Sentiment in Figure 3). Although it is difficult to make stronger interpretations with a small number of documents, the fact that they are spread over a number of years helps us to arrive at a weak conclusion.

A number of additional analyses are possible. Of these, the interesting ones are analyses that allow comparison of sentiment and confidence across multiple stakeholders. For example, it may be possible to distinguish trends where some of the stakeholders' perceptions may mirror, suggesting possibilities for building coalitions as well as for the purpose of managing expectations across stakeholders. These analyses are ongoing.

## 6  Conclusion and Next Steps

Enterprise architecture involves not only the description of static phenomena but also the active, change-oriented efforts for re-architecting an enterprise. The duration and resources for these efforts often tend to be very large. Research efforts, therefore, can examine the documents and evidence that these efforts leave behind to understand how they take place and learn from these. The central motivation of this research was to explore how Sentiment and Confidence analysis techniques based on historical analysis of documents that can provide clues to how different stakeholders may participate and engage with the re-architecting effort. The research methodology we used for this purpose was the application of a simple text-mining process that allows longitudinal analysis, described as a case study.

Although the analyses continue based on the data and tagging described in the paper, the preliminary results based on the measures outlined suggest that longitudinal analysis of Sentiment and Confidence as well as comparison of these across stakeholder groups can provide clues for understanding how the re-architecting process progresses. It is possible to extend and interpret the results based on an understanding of stakeholder roles and how difference stakeholders may participate in the effort. Another possible application of the results may be to consider how these sentiments and confidence measures provide warnings of impending problems. For example, notions such as systemic risks (Carlo 2004) and risk society (Beck 1992) have been suggested that expand our understanding of risk. However, this literature positions the source of risk as external and continues to negate the endogenous nature of risk (Lyytinen et al. 1998). The ideas in this paper suggest another possibility.

Some caveats are, however, in order. The analyses we have presented rely on measures of sentiment and confidence that may be refined. The analysis to compute these measures can also accommodate more sophisticated text processing techniques with the sets available as part of the General Inquirer (see http://www.wjh.harvard.edu/~inquirer/homecat.htm) as well as more recent parsing and rule-based mechanisms. The most interesting aspects of our ongoing work, however, stem from the myriad of analyses that are possible with such historical data and how these analyses can lead to interesting results for understanding re-architecting efforts. As we continue this stream of research, we hope that we will be able to uncover additional findings that allow use of multiple confirmatory as well as competing cases. These remain on our future research agenda.

## Acknowledgements

We would like to express our appreciation to Karin Lamb McConnell for her able assistance for creating the corpus of text used in this research.

## References

[1] Agranoff, R., McGuire, M.: American federalism and the search for models of management. Public Administration Review 16, 18–41 (2001)

[2] Agranoff, R., McGuire, M.: Multi-Network Management: Collaboration and the Hollow State. Journal of Public Administration Research and Theory 8(1), 67–91 (1998)

[3] Agranoff, R., McGuire, M.: Managing in Network Settings. Policy Studies Review 8(1), 67–91 (1999)

[4] Aaltonen, K.: Project stakeholder analysis as an environmental interpretation process. International Journal of Project Management (in Press, 2010)

[5] Beck, U.: From Industrial Society to the Risk Society: Questions of Survival, Social Structure and Ecological Enlightenment. Theory, Culture & Society 9(1), 97–123 (1992)

[6] Brownsword, L., Fisher, D., Morris, E., Smith, J., Kirwan, P.: System-of-Systems Navigator: An Approach for Managing System-of-Systems Interoperability. Technical Note CMU/SEI-2006-TN-019 (2006)

[7] Carlo, J.L., Lyytinen, K., Boland, R.J.: Systemic Risk, IT Artifacts, and High Reliability Organizations: A Case of Constructing a Radical Architecture. Working Papers on Information Systems, Sprouts, Case Western Reserve University, USA, vol. 4(4) (2004), http://sprouts.aisnet.org/4-4

[8] Charette, R.N.: Why Software Fails. IEEE Spectrum (2005)

[9] Flyvbjerg, B., et al.: Megaprojects and Risk: An Anatomy of Ambition. Cambridge University Press, Cambridge (2003)

[10] Gardiner, P.: Management performance challenges facing IRS FY2003 (October 15, 2002), http://www.treas.gov/tigta/management/management_fy2003.htm

[11] Gardiner, P.: Management performance challenges facing IRS FY2004 (October 15, 2003), http://www.treas.gov/tigta/management/management_fy2004.htm

[12] Gardiner, P.: Management performance challenges facing IRS FY2005 (October 26, 2004), http://www.treas.gov/tigta/management/management_fy2005-long.htm

[13] Gardiner, P.: Annual assessment of the Internal Revenue Service's Business Systems Modernization Program (August 10, 2005), http://www.treas.gov/tigta/auditreports/2005reports/200520102fr.pdf

[14] George, J.R.: Management performance challenges facing IRS FY2006 (October 27, 2005), http://www.treas.gov/tigta/management/management_fy2006.htm

[15] George, J.R.: Management performance challenges facing IRS FY2006 (October 2, 2006), http://www.treas.gov/tigta/management/management_fy2007.htm

[16] George, J.R.: Management performance challenges facing IRS FY2008 (October 29, 2007), http://www.treas.gov/tigta/management/management_fy2008.htm

[17] George, J.R.: Management performance challenges facing IRS FY2009 (October 15, 2008), http://www.treas.gov/tigta/management/management_fy2009.htm

[18] George, J.R.: Management performance challenges facing IRS FY2010 (October 15, 2009), http://www.treas.gov/tigta/management/management_fy2010.htm

[19] Gregory, M.L., et al.: User-directed sentiment analysis: visualizing the affective content of documents. In: Proceedings of the Workshop on Sentiment and Subjectivity in Text, pp. 23–30. ACL, Sydney (2006)

[20] Innes, J., Booher, D.: Consensus building and complex adaptive systems: A framework for evaluating collaborative planning American Planning Association. Journal of the American Planning Association 65(4), 412 (Autumn 1999)

[21] Internal Revenue Service: Award/Contract between the Internal Revenue Service and Computer Sciences Corporation (December 9, 1998), http://www.irs.gov/pub/irs-procure/prime-contract.pdf

[22] Internal Revenue Service: The agency, its mission and statutory authority (November 5, 2007), http://www.irs.gov/irs/article/0,,id=98141,00.html

[23] Internal Revenue Service: Terence V. Milholland to serve as IRS Chief Technology Officer (November 15, 2008), http://www.irs.gov/pub/irs-news/ir-08-129.pdf

[24] Kettl, D.: Managing Boundaries in American Administration: The Collaboration Imperative. Public Administration Review 66, 10 (2006)

[25] Langley, A.: Strategies for Theorizing from Process Data. The Academy of Management Review 24(4), 691–710 (1999)

[26] Lyytinen, K., Mathiassen, L., Ropponen, J.: Attention Shaping and Software Risk – A Categorical Analysis of Four Classical Risk Management Approaches. Information System Research 9(3), 233–255 (1998)

[27] Markus, L.M., Robey, D.: Information Technology and Organizational Change: Causal Structure in Theory and Research. Management Science 34(5), 583–598 (1988)

[28] Nowell, B.: Out of Sync and Unaware? Exploring the Effects of Problem Frame Alignment and Discordance in Community Collaboratives. Journal of Public Administration Research and Theory 20(1), 91 (2010)

[29] Phillips, M.: Annual assessment of the Internal Revenue Service's Business Systems Modernization Program (August 24, 2007), http://www.treas.gov/tigta/auditreports/2007reports/200720121fr.pdf

[30] Phillips, M.: Annual assessment of the Internal Revenue Service's Business Systems Modernization Program (September 14, 2009), http://www.treas.gov/tigta/auditreports/2009reports/200920136fr.pdf

[31] Rossotti, C.: Statement of Charles O. Rossotti, Commissioner of Internal Revenue Service, before the Senate Finance Committee (January 28, 1998), http://www.irs.gov/pub/irs-news/ir-98-3.pdf

[32] Sahin, B.: Factors influencing effectiveness of interorganizational networks among crisis management organizations: A comparative perspective. University of Central Florida (2009)

[33] Umapathy, K., Purao, S., Bagby, J.: Analyzing the Processes behind Web Service Standards Development. In: 8th e-Business Workshop, Phoenix, AZ (December 2009)

[34] U.S. Department of the Treasury: Duties & functions of the U.S. Department of the Treasury (October 23, 2008), http://www.ustreas.gov/education/duties/

[35] Watts, L., Groen, Y., Matsubara, K., Hovey, J., Whittle, M.: Internal Revenue Service Restructuring and Reform Act of 1998 (2005), http://www.pmstax.com/gen/bul19808.shtml

[36] Watts, L., Groen, Y., Matsubara, K., Hovey, J., Whittle, M.: Internal Revenue Service Restructuring and Reform Act of 1998 (2005),
http://www.pmstax.com/gen/bull9808.shtml

[37] Weber, R.: Basic content analysis. SAGE, London (1996)

[38] Williams, D.: Management performance challenges facing IRS FY2000 (December 1, 1999),
http://www.treas.gov/tigta/management/management_fy2000.htm

[39] Yin, R.K.: Case Study Research. Sage Publications, Thousand Oaks (2003)

# A Conceptual Framework for Enterprise Architecture Design

Sabine Buckl, Florian Matthes, Sascha Roth,
Christopher Schulz, and Christian M. Schweda

Technische Universität München (TUM)
Chair for Informatics 19 (sebis)
Boltzmannstr. 3, 85748 Garching bei München, Germany
{buckls,matthes,rothsa,schulzc,schweda}@in.tum.de

**Abstract.** An ambiguous terminology as well as a lack of clarity prevail in information systems research when focusing on enterprise architecture (EA) and its corresponding management function. Sound definitions for key terms in the field of EA design, i.e. strategies, principles, and goals, are too often used interchangeably with slightly different meaning. Addressing this situation, the present article proposes a conceptual framework for EA design that covers the aforementioned terms and organizes them along two dimensions, namely their underlying EA conceptualization and their role in the design process. The framework is exemplified and mirrored against state-of-the-art literature in the realm of EA and the corresponding management function. Finally, the article sketches further research trends centering around the design of an EA.

**Keywords:** enterprise architecture, enterprise architecture management, conceptual framework, strategy, goal, principle, standard.

## 1 Introduction

In the past decade *enterprise architecture* (EA) and its corresponding management function have gained considerable attention from the academic and practical audience. With the main objective of the management function to align business and IT its management subject is the enterprise's architecture which according to the ISO/IEC 42010 (2007) [11], can be defined as "the fundamental organization of [the enterprise] embodied in its components, their relationships to each other, and to the environment, and the principles guiding its design and evolution". Distinct states of an EA are typically developed during EA management, the *current state* describing the status quo, the *target state*, forming an envisioned long-term perspective, and intermediate *planned states*, representing the medium-term objectives to be achieved. Regarding both planned and target states, the business represents the main 'driver' of the organizational change whereas projects are the 'implementors'. In order to ensure a managed evolution (cf. Murer et al. in [15]), projects have to be evaluated according to the principles guiding an EA's design and evolution.

E. Proper et al. (Eds.): TEAR 2010, LNBIP 70, pp. 44–56, 2010.

Albeit the frequent references to concepts as *principle, vision,* and *strategy* in recent EA management-related literature (see e.g. [6,20,23]), concise and tangible definitions as well as classifications are still missing. Focusing for example on the term EA principle, existing sources [21,25] typically apply related terminologies in an ambiguous manner while highlighting the importance of principles in the same breath. Especially, the EA management community lacks clarity how EA principles relate to the also frequently used terms *vision* and *strategy* or the often synonymously used term *standard*. Furthermore, the relationship between the aforementioned terms and the *projects* realizing enterprise transformation is of interest. These terminological unclarities drive the two core research questions of this article:

- What are major concepts for the design of an enterprise architecture and how they are defined?
- How those concepts embed in an abstract design framework for EAs?

The present article seeks to answer these questions by providing a framework that both helps to define and to understand the interplay of these terms. The framework is based on the prefabrics of the OMG's Business Motivation Model [16], Simon's science of the artificial [19], and the work on language communities of Kamlah and Lorenzen in [13] (see Section 2). The elaborated structure is further linked to the approach of the managed evolution already evoked above (Section 3). Afterwards, the framework developed is used to revisit the state-of-the-art in EA management literature in Section 4. Based on the analysis results future research directions in the area of EA management are derived and discussed in the concluding Section 5.

## 2   Principles in the Context of Management

The management of the EA is an activity intended to evolve the architecture as well as to control the evolution thereof. In this sense EA management can be understood a design activity (cf. van der Raadt and van Vliet in [24]) targeting the enterprise in a comprehensive manner. Enterprise architects (*designers*), with a planned state (*end*) in mind, search for the *means* by which the EA will achieve those aims. As part of this search the architects develop different plan scenarios of the EA and evaluate these with respect to the achievement of the desired end. The design activity may thereby be understood as a purely 'mental' one operating on a *mental model* of the enterprise also incorporating the according *means-end*-relationships.

In [19] Simon calls for a more formal understanding of design involving an imperative style of logic. In particular he proposes to operationalize the means-end-relationships behind any design problem into logical statements relating

**command variables** describing objects (architecture elements) that may be changed by design activities,

**fixed parameters** describing architectural properties as well as environmental aspects that cannot be changed by design activities,

**constraints** limiting the space of changes that can be made by a design activity, and

**a utility function** evaluating a designed architecture in respect to the (experienced) utility for its stakeholders.

In above terms the search for the planned state to pursue may be reformulated as 'find values for the command variables fulfilling the given constraints in the context of the fixed parameters that they best satisfy the utility function'. For the field of EA management such reformulation may at first seem a worthless exercise, as finding and defining formal command variables may be regarded a highly sophisticated and not easy to accomplish task. Nevertheless, the core distinction between command variables, constraints, and a utility function can be beneficially applied to understand, distinguish, and relate concepts as principles, strategies, and goals.

Complementing above considerations, we briefly revisit the notion of the mental model as essential part of addressing design problems. Every enterprise architect (as designer of the EA) uses a mental model of the enterprise to plan and evaluate the corresponding design alternatives. This model covers a specific area-of-interest, i.e. *concern* in terms of the ISO/IEC 42010 (2007), in the overall architecture of the enterprise. In line with Buckl et al. (cf. [3]) such concern may on the one hand be identified with a specific *conceptualization* of the enterprise, i.e. with a problem- and designer-specific classification of relevant elements of the enterprise. On the other hand a concern commits to a specific *filter* determining which parts of the enterprise are considered relevant. Two mental models as employed by two enterprise architects may hence differ in respect to both the conceptualization, i.e. the classification of elements, and the filtering, i.e. the selection of elements. In order to form the basis for a collaborative EA management conducted by a group of enterprise architects and other EAstakeholders, these people have to agree on a shared conceptualization. They have to be in one *linguistic community* (in terms of Kamlah and Lorenzen [13]) in order to be able to communicate their architecture understanding to collaboratively design and evolve the EA.

In the context of EA design activities more formal conceptualizations of the enterprise are widely used to facilitate communication between different EA stakeholders. These conceptualizations are mostly reflected in corresponding EA modeling languages, more precisely their underlying *information models*[1]. These models are conceptual models committing to an agreed conceptualization (cf. Buckl et al. in [3]) of the EA or parts thereof as relevant in respect to important stakeholders and their design problems. These stakeholders form the corresponding linguistic community for which instantiations of the information model are accessible. In the light of the above discussions we devise a framework for distinguishing and relating the different concepts as discussed in Section 1. This framework builds on two axes, namely one considering the level of operationalization (*mental conceptualization* vs. *information model*) and one distinguishing

---

[1] The meta-models backing an EA modeling language are in line with Buckl et al. (cf. [2]) named information models here.

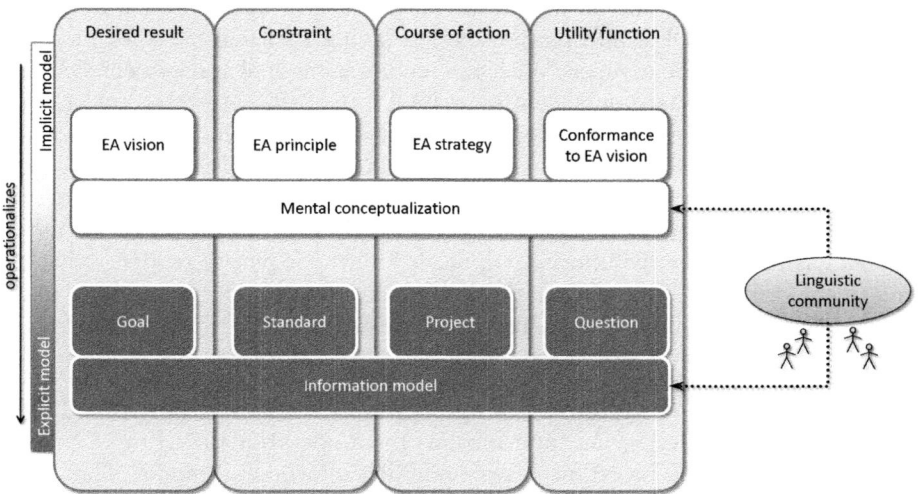

**Fig. 1.** Conceptual framework for EA design

between *desired result*, *course of action*, *utility function*, and *constraints*. Figure 1 outlines this framework and shows how the different concepts can be related therein.

Against the background of the framework we apply definitions for the different concepts as follows:

**An EA vision** is a distant target representing an ideal state, i.e. an implicit model and understanding of a target state of an EA. This aligns with the definition given by Lankhorst et al. in [14], saying that the "[EA] vision states an 'image of the future' and the values the enterprise holds".

**An EA principle** constrains and guides the design of the EA (cf. [18]) and may in turn provide justification for decision-making throughout an EA (cf. [22]). In general, principles are self-restraint and not externally obliged, e.g. by law in terms of compliances.

**An EA strategy** outlines a series of means (activities) to pursue a desired end, i.e. a dedicated target state of an EA. Refraining the complementary definition given in the OMG's Business Motivation Model (BMM) [16] a strategy is an "accepted [...] approach to achieve [desired ends], given the environmental constraints and risks".

**Conformance to EA vision** describes an intuitive understanding for the degree to which the current or a planned state of the EA matches the EA vision.

All the concepts mentioned before build on an informal and intuitive understanding as incorporated in the mental model of the corresponding linguistic community, e.g. the enterprise architects as designers of the EA. Refraining above argument on design in the EA context being a collaborative activity, these mental models, more precisely their backing conceptualizations, are frequently complemented with EA information models laying a formal basis for modeling the EA in an explicit manner. With the embracingness of the subject EA, it is sensible to assume that not the entire architecture of the enterprise but only relevant areas are covered by an information model. The decision on relevance may therein pertain to cover the areas-of-interest mirroring the visions, principles and strategies, but also to keep low the expenses for gathering and maintaining the information about the contained concepts. Put in other words, an information model has to balance the information needs and the expenses related to gathering this information. As consequence thereof, the mental concepts outlined above may only be partially operationalized to concrete pendants described below:

**A Goal** is a "statement about a state or condition of the enterprise to be brought about or sustained through appropriate means" (cf. [16]). In this sense, a goal describes an (intermediary) *end* operationalizing the EA vision or a part thereof, based on a corresponding information model. The goal is thereby "defined for an object [...] with respect to various models of quality [...]", i.e. is attached to a specific object in this model in terms of Basili et al. [1].

**A Standard** describes a "predefined design norm" based on principles and standards defined earlier (cf. [10]). In line with this argumentation standards describe a particular interpretation of an EA principle with respect to the information model.

**A Project** is concerned with the fulfillment of a goal. Consequently, any effort within a project should contribute to a goal, based on an information model. Thus, a project may be EA related in terms that it influences the EA, or an explicit EA transformation project.

**A Question** or a set thereof "is used to characterize the way the assessment/achievement of a specific goal is going to be performed" (cf. [1]). This means that a question measures the achievement of a goal based on the conceptualization mirrored in an information model.

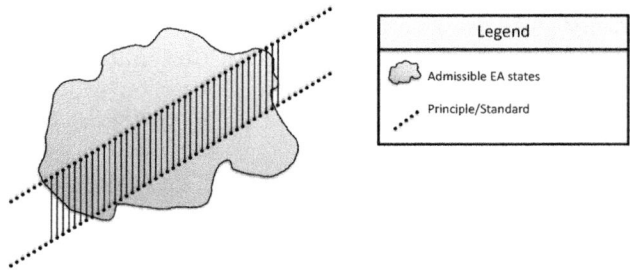

**Fig. 2.** EA principles constraining the EA design space

Both, principles and standards may be formulated in two different ways, namely as guidelines (respectively recommendations) or as restrictions (cf. [18]). In either way, a principle or a standard restricts the design space (cf. Figure 2), i.e. the set of accepted states, although the level of strictness may vary. Revisiting the relationships between a principle and the according standards one might say, that the standards operationalize the principle, while the latter provides the underlying rationale. The link between principle and vision is a more delicate one. While we in general can assume that the EA principles and EA vision do not contradict each other, i.e. that the vision is admissible against the background of the established principles, the same does not necessarily hold for standards and goals.

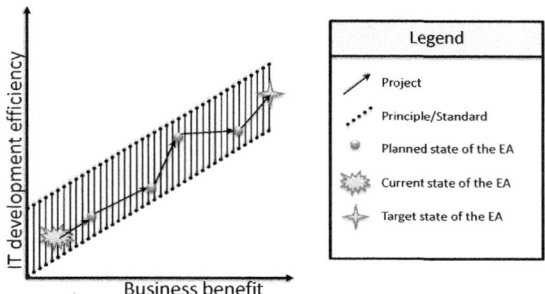

**Fig. 3.** EA principles in the paradigm of managed evolution

Figure 3 illustrates the role of EA principles within the paradigm of managed evolution [15] describing an iterative and controlled approach of EA development within multiple transformation projects. The EA evolves over time between the guidelines and constraints set by effective EA principles. In contrast to [15], we identified that these 'side rails' are manifested in EA principles as well as standards guiding on the one hand the evolution of the EA, and restricting on the other hand the possible EA states taken to evolve to an EAtarget state.

Over time, e.g. due to an increasing amount of technologies, the design space of EA management with regards to the set of admissible EA states widens. Since EA principles are static, this observation let us conclude the effectiveness of EA principles is degenerating on the long run. In conclusion, any applied standard, i.e. operationalized EA principle, has to generate feedback such that EA principles become dynamic and thus can evolve over time aligning to the needs of the EA evolution.

## 3   Exemplifying the Approach

Making the above conceptual framework more explicit, an example leaning against Murer et al. [15] is provided in the this section. In Murer's example, a swiss bank has the EA vision (reflected in a target state of the EA) which supports the continuous implementation of new business requirements under high cost and time-to-market pressure. Furthermore, the EA vision states that IT systems must remain available, reliable, and secure as well as to assure effectiveness and economy of the business at the same time.

In our example, we assume that the bank has one important EA principle, namely to concentrate development competences of the IT departments. This principle is operationalized via a standard that defines a restricted set of programming languages to be used, namely Java, C++, and COBOL. With the EA vision of having an easily adaptable and flexible EA, the corresponding strategy is to transform the EA, more precisely the application landscape, into a service-oriented landscape that makes use of external services and service outsourcing where sensibly possible. This strategy has been pursued for some time by different projects that were able to implement service-orientation in certain parts of the overall EA.

At a certain point in time, the swiss bank decides to offer its customers an 'app' enabling mobile online banking which induces a positive influence on the bank's distribution and communication channel. In this vein, business benefit also reflected in the bank's overall reputation for cutting-edge technology is increased. With this short time goal set, resources for a new project are allocated targeting the development of such mobile application. Since the mobile application requires Objective C as the unique programming language, the above defined programming language standard is violated at the expense of short term business benefit. Figure 4 illustrates the impact of the 'mobile app'-project on the overall state of the EA.

After the successful completion of the project introducing a mobile application, a follow-up project is planned. This project replaces the mobile application developed in-house with a commercial of the shelf product leveraging the *Home Banking Computer Interface* (HBCI). In doing so, the application is reworked in a way that the actual development in Objective C is performed by a third party resulting in the conformance of the programming language standard.

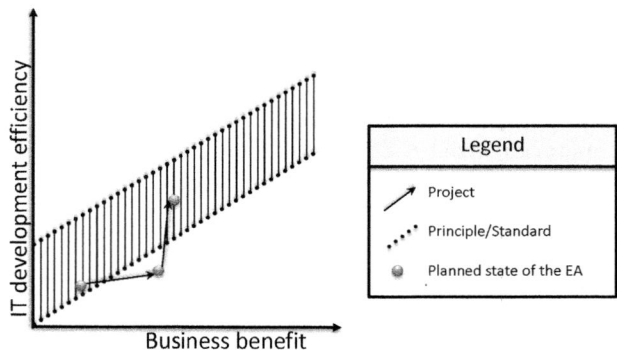

**Fig. 4.** EA evolution with a standard deviating project

# 4    Revisiting the State-of-the-Art in EA Management Literature

In this section, six prominent approaches in the area of EA and the respective management function are discussed on the basis of the conceptual framework as presented in Section 2. Thereby, the terminology as employed in the original sources is used and compared to the concepts and understanding presented in this paper. Regarding the research method, the approach of hermeneutics (cf. [9]) is applied helping to interpret and map the identified concepts found in literature to the corresponding framework elements.

In his recent work [5,6], Stelzer conducts an in-depth literature analysis on EA principles ranging from frameworks for EA and textbooks, to journals and conference publications. The author afterwards systematizes the investigated sources by decomposing an architecture principle into objects, context and description, scope of application, and its delimitation from other forms of principles. While he points out that there exists so far non-explained relationships between EA goals, principles, as well as means of their application, Stelzer refrains from providing a summarizing definition of these terms as well as from giving information how their relationship to each other is characterized. Notwithstanding, the author describes that architecture principles are embedded in a network of associated principles and highlights the fact, that their existence, differentiation, designation, and interrelation is contingent on the specific enterprise setting. Based on his profound literature analysis, Stelzer motivates to consider principles in a broader context and highlights that they are embedded in rationale and implications. However, by leaving out how these two concepts can be linked to an EA vision or EA strategy and by focusing on goals and EA principles, he refrains from explaining the broader context a principle is part of. Hence, additional concepts as proposed by the framework, e.g. different linguistic communities, projects, and questions are not examined by the author. Besides principles pertaining solely to the EA as indicated in both publications' titles (cf. [5,6]), the author also implicitly refers to principles related to the management of an EA, IT, and business.

In *The Open Group Architecture Framework* (TOGAF) [21] is a prominent framework for developing an EA. Following the *Architecture Development Method* (ADM) which is subdivided into nine phases, an architecture vision describing "how the new capability will meet the business goals and strategic objectives and address the stakeholder concerns when implemented" is established in the first phase. Thereby TOGAF denotes an enterprise mission, vision, strategy, and goals as key elements of an architecture vision and points out that it provides "a first-cut, high-level description of the baseline and target Architectures, covering the business, data, application, and technology domains.". In addition, the vision also contains architecture principles which are defined as "general rules and guidelines, intended to be enduring and seldom amended, that inform and support the way in which an organization sets about fulfilling its mission". In differentiating between principles on enterprise-, IT-, and architecture level, the framework also proposes a specific format for defining architecture principles consisting of name, statement, rationale, and implications. Furthermore, architecture principles as subset of IT principles, are subdivided into a) principles that govern the architecture process and b) principles which govern the implementation of the architecture. Whereas former refer to the management of an EA, latter center around the guidance for designing and developing information systems. In this vein, the misleading term "architecture principles" in TOGAF rather pertains to main guidelines considering the management of an EA and not the elements of an EA itself. Furthermore, business principles, as a fourth type of principles are introduced separately and are linked uniquely to an architecture project, which also has to take current goals and strategic drivers into account. While TOGAF does not make any distinction between an implicit and explicit level, it also lacks in defining and creating concrete and consistent relationships among those concepts. For instance, the framework introduces the term blueprint as "collection of the actual standards and specifications" but leaves out to define the link regarding EA principles and strategy. Additional elements being part of the conceptual framework suggested above are not accounted for by TOGAF.

The approach of multi-perspective enterprise modeling (MEMO) of Frank [7] provides a framework consisting of a set of special purpose modeling languages, which can be leveraged to support different perspectives (strategy, organization, and information system) as well as various aspects relevant for enterprise modeling (EM). In their recent work, Frank et al. [8] elaborate requirements for a method aiming at the design and utilization of indicator systems within an enterprise environment. In leveraging the core concepts of SCORE-ML which have been embedded into the existing EM method supporting in turn the modeling of processes, resources, and goals, the authors associate indicators with the relevant business context. In the corresponding SCORE-ML meta model, indicators are directly related to goals which they are representing. Moreover, goals may be organized into a multi-layered hierarchy. Further concepts as proposed by the framework like strategy, principles, and visions of an EA as well as their operationalized counterparts (e.g. project, standard, and question) are neither considered by the SCORE-ML method nor embedded in the meta model.

Österle et al. [17] suggest a core-business-metamodel subsuming the main concepts of the strategy, organization, and system level. In depicting the relationships between concepts on these levels through a model which is restricted to the core elements of a business, the model supports the implementation of the St. Gallen's business engineering approach. The approach has been proven successful throughout more than 1000 consulting projects and is regularly re-applied for scientific publications (see e.g. [4]). Regarding the model in detail, goals as part of an enterprise's strategy are specified on a business level, although a strategy is only modeled implicitly in assigning distinct classes to the strategic level. Further concepts of above presented framework (e.g. EA principles, vision, project, and questions) are not in the scope of the model.

*Control Objectives for Information and related Technology* (COBIT) represents a prominent framework for IT management created by the Information Systems Audit and Control Association (ISACA) in close cooperation with the

IT Governance Institute (ITGI) [12]. The framework is focused on what is required to achieve adequate management and control of IT, and is positioned on an abstract level. By being composed of four domains which are subdivided into 34 IT processes each consisting of a set of activities, COBIT provides a reference process model and common language for everyone in an enterprise to view and manage IT activities. In creating and explaining a linkage between an enterprise strategy, business goals for IT, IT goals, EA, and the IT scorecard, the framework emphasizes that an enterprise strategy influences the IT resources and capabilities, thus the EA. Furthermore, COBIT proposes an informal relationship between business-, IT-, process-, and activity goals which can be measured via the corresponding performance metrics driving in turn the respective higher-level goal. Although the framework states that suggested standards and good practices "are most useful when applied as a set of principles and as a starting point for tailoring specific procedures" COBIT does not include (EA) principles. Moreover, neither a formalized linkage between strategy and related goals is provided, nor a distinction between different levels of operationalization reflected in the different types of models is given. Additional concepts which are part of the presented framework (e.g. EA strategy, vision, project) are not addressed by COBIT.

A comprehensive picture of EA-related concepts including their definitions is provided by Schekkerman [18]. According to Schekkerman, a standard "is an agreement on how things should be done, or, in other words, a rule (or set of rules) on which an agreement exists". While a principle is defined on a higher level of abstraction by expressing "an idea, a message (culture / behavior) or value that comes from corporate vision, strategies, and business drivers, experience or from knowledge of a subject". Schekkerman also emphasizes, that principles (which similar to TOGAF consist of a name, statement, rationale, and implications) govern the business and organization as well as the development and implementation of the EA. However, the author does not consistently distinguish between the level of operationalization and means-end-relationships, as proposed by the framework presented in Section 2. In addition, Schekkerman speaks of a general vision and strategy referring to the main drivers and requirements of an enterprise but does not derive the according EA concepts and their pendants.

## 5   Future Research Questions

In this article, we devised a conceptual framework for EA design helping to overcome the ambiguity of terminology in the research field. In distinguishing between desired result, constraint, course of action, and utility function as well as an implicit and explicit model, we presented major concepts, defined them systematically, and finally sketched a framework into which these concepts embed. In doing so, the article leverages the prominent approach of the managed evolution of application landscapes in order to exemplify the elaborated framework.

As part of the article, the term linguistic community was introduced as a group which continuously communicates their architecture understanding to collaboratively design and evolve the EA. When taking a closer look on the framework elements being related to the implicit model, it becomes obvious that distinct groups share a different understanding resulting in deviating interpretations of the concept's instances. For example, the same EA principle can be operationalized by different corresponding standards taking the context like terminology, knowledge, and experience of the according linguistic community into consideration. Further research could focus on the manner how the different implicit model elements, i.e. EA vision, principle, strategy, and conformance to the vision, are made explicit depending on the community they are exposed to.

In the course of our literature review, we noticed that only few sources suggest utility function(s) in order to evaluate the fulfillment of the desired results given a specific set of constraints while following a certain course of action. Not only this type of functions could help to assess the actual goal achievement, it would also allow for a profound statistical analysis in addition to an internal and external comparison. Some approaches, like the one of COBIT [12], already motivate and propose textual questions targeting at the actual goal fulfillment, but fall short when it comes to the incorporation of principles and standards restricting the admissible EA states.

Regarding the various relationships among the framework's concepts, further research is required in order to refine the different interrelations. Thereby, one has to consider both, relations between concepts residing in the same as well as concepts being part of different models. In doing so, generic methodologies could be elaborated transforming elements of the implicit model to their explicit pendants. Furthermore, the incorporation of the framework's concepts within an explicit model longs for further investigation. For instance, the question arises how to easily integrate different EA standards representing guidelines and constraints in an existing information model by simultaneously striving for a generic and reusable approach.

Lastly, one has to take into consideration that during the EA design process each enterprise pursues several goals by also being bound to a variety of constraints at the same time. In most cases, different courses of actions can be taken while applying a different set of appropriate utility functions. From this perspective, multi-objective optimization coping with the increased complexity of the problem may deserve further investigations including the identification of an appropriate Pareto optimum.

# References

1. Basili, V.R., Caldiera, G., Rombach, H.D.: The Goal Question Metric Approach. Wiley, Chichester (1994)
2. Buckl, S., Ernst, A.M., Lankes, J., Schneider, K., Schweda, C.M.: A pattern based approach for constructing enterprise architecture management information models. In: Wirtschaftsinformatik 2007, Karlsruhe, Germany, pp. 145–162. Universitätsverlag Karlsruhe (2007)

3. Buckl, S., Krell, S., Schweda, C.M.: A formal approach to architectural descriptions – refining the iso standard 42010. In: 6th International Workshop on Cooperation & Interoperability – Architecture & Ontology, CIAO 2010 (2010)
4. Dinter, B., Winter, R. (eds.): Integrierte Informationslogistik (Business Engineering) (German Edition), 1st edn. Springer, Heidelberg (2008)
5. Stelzer, D.: Enterprise Architecture Principles: Literature Review and Research Directions. In: 4th Workshop on Trends in Enterprise Architecture Research (TEAR), Stockholm, Sweden (2009)
6. Stelzer, D.: Prinzipien für Unternehmensarchitekturen - Grundlagen und Systematisierung. In: Schumann, M., Kolbe, L.M., Breitner, M.H., Frerichs, A. (eds.) Multikonferenz Wirtschaftsinformatik (MKWI 2010), Göttingen, Germany, pp. 55–66 (2010)
7. Frank, U.: Multi-perspective enterprise modeling (memo) – conceptual framework and modeling languages. In: Proceedings of the 35th Annual Hawaii International Conference on System Sciences (HICSS 2002), Washington, DC, USA, pp. 1258–1267 (2002)
8. Frank, U., Heise, D., Kattenstroth, H., Schauer, H.: Designing and utilising business indicator systems within enterprise models – outline of a method. In: Modellierung betrieblicher Informationssysteme (MobIS 2008) – Modellierung zwischen SOA und Compliance Management, Saarbrücken, Germany, November 27-28 (2008)
9. Gadamer, H.-G.: Wahrheit und Methode – Grundzüge einer philosophischen Hermeneutik, 3rd edn. J.C.B. Mohr, Tübingen (1975)
10. Hoogervorst, J.A.P.: Enterprise Governance and Enterprise Engineering, 1st edn. The Enterprise Engineering Series. Springer, Heidelberg (February 2009)
11. International Organization for Standardization. ISO/IEC 42010:2007 Systems and software engineering – Recommended practice for architectural description of software-intensive systems (2007)
12. IT Governance Institute: Framework Control Objectives Management Guidelines Maturity Models (2009), http://www.isaca.org/Knowledge-Center/cobit (cited 2010-06-18)
13. Kamlah, W., Lorenzen, P.: Logische Propädeutik: Vorschule des vernünftigen Redens, 3rd edn. Metzler, Stuttgart (1996)
14. Lankhorst, M.: Enterprise Architecture at Work: Modelling, Communication and Analysis. Springer, Heidelberg (2005)
15. Murer, S., Worms, C., Furrer, F.J.: Managed evolution. Informatik Spektrum 31(6), 537–547 (2008)
16. Object Management Group. Business Motivation Model 1.1. (2010), http://www.omg.org/spec/BMM/1.1/ (cited 2010-06-15)
17. Österle, H., Winter, R., Hoening, F., Kurpjuweit, S., Osl, P.: Business Engineering: Core-Business-Metamodell. Wisu – Das Wirtschaftsstudium 36(2), 191–194 (2007)
18. Schekkerman, J.: Enterprise Architecture Good Practices Guide – How to Manage the Enterprise Architecture Practice. Trafford Publishing, Victoria (2008)
19. Simon, H.A.: The Sciences of the Artificial, 3rd edn. MIT Press, Cambridge (1996)
20. Steininger, K., Riedl, R., Roithmayr, F., Mertens, P.: Moden und Trends in Wirtschaftsinformatik und Information Systems. Wirtschaftsinformatik 51(6), 478–495 (2009)
21. The Open Group. TOGAF "Enterprise Edition" Version 9 (2009), http://www.togaf.org (cited 2010-02-25)
22. The Open Group. TOGAF Version 9 - A Manual, 9th edn. Van Haren Publishing (2009)

23. van Bommel, P., Buitenhuis, P.G., Stijn, J., Hoppenbrouwers, S.J.B.A., Proper, E.H.: Architecture Principles - A Regulative Perspective on Enterprise Architecture. In: Reichert, M., Strecker, S., Turowski, K. (eds.) 1st International Workshop on Enterprise Modelling and Information Systems Architectures (EMISA), Bonn, Germany, pp. 47–60 (2007)
24. van der Raadt, B., van Vliet, H.: Designing the enterprise architecture function. In: Becker, S., Plasil, F., Reussner, R. (eds.) QoSA 2008. LNCS, vol. 5281, pp. 103–118. Springer, Heidelberg (2008)
25. Winter, R., Fischer, R.: Essential layers, artifacts, and dependencies of enterprise architecture. Journal of Enterprise Architecture 3(2), 7–18 (2007)

# The Roles of Principles in Enterprise Architecture

H.A. (Erik) Proper[1,2] and D. (Danny) Greefhorst[3]

[1] Public Research Centre Henri Tudor, Luxembourg
[2] Radboud University Nijmegen, Nijmegen, The Netherlands
[3] ArchiXL, Amersfoort, The Netherlands

**Abstract.** Key concepts in enterprise architecture include concerns, principles, models, views and frameworks. While most of these concepts have received ample attention in research, the concept of principles has not been studied much yet. In this paper, we therefore specifically focus on the role of principles in the field of enterprise architecture, where we position enterprise architecture as a means to direct enterprise transformations.

In practice, many different types of architecture principles are used. At the same time, principles are referred to by different names, including architecture principles, design principles, and IT policies. The primary goal of this paper is, therefore, to arrive at a conceptual framework to more clearly clarify and position these different types.

The paper starts with a discussion on enterprise architecture as a means to govern enterprise transformation. This provides a framework to position the different types of principles, and highlight their roles in enterprise transformations.

## 1 Introduction

As discussed in [1], key concepts in the field of enterprise architecture include *concerns*, *principles*, *models*, *views* and *frameworks*. Ample research has been conducted on architecture frameworks, architecture modelling languages [2, 3], model analysis [4, 5], as well as viewpoints and concerns [6, 7, 8]. In this paper we turn our focus to the concept of *principles* and its role in the field of enterprise architecture. Given that principles have not received a lot of research attention [9], there is a need to better understand their essense.

Several approaches to enterprise architecture position principles as an important ingredient [10, 11, 1, 12, 13], while some even go as far as to position principles as being the essence of architecture [14]. At the same time, initial case studies [15, 16, 17, 18, 19, 20, 21, 22, 23, 24, 25] indicate there to be a wide variation in the actual use of principles. The primary aim of this paper is therefore to arrive at a first version of a conceptual framework which more clearly identifies and positions the different types of principles.

The framework presented in this paper is the first iteration in a design science [26] driven research effort in which we aim to more clearly define the concept of architecture principles, and develop an associated methodology for defining and describing architecture principles. This first iteration, provides a synthesis of existing views on enterprise architecture and enterprise engineering [27, 1, 14, 13].

E. Proper et al. (Eds.): TEAR 2010, LNBIP 70, pp. 57–70, 2010.

The remainder of this paper is structured as follows. Before we are able to sensibly explore the different types of principles, and their roles in enterprise transformations, Section 2 offers a review of our understanding of the fundamental purpose of architecture as a means to direct enterprise transformation. In Section 3, we then provide a conceptual framework of the different types of principles that can be discerned within our field.

## 2   Architecture as a Means to Govern Enterprise Transformations

In line with [1], we take the perspective that enterprise architecture should play a pivotal role in governing the continuous improvement process of an enterprise. In order to better understand the governing role of enterprise architecture, this section positions architecture as a means to govern enterprise transformations. As we will see, principles are the key means to govern the direction of the transformation of an enterprise.

In our view, governing enterprise transformations first and foremost entails the perspective on an enterprise as a purposely designed and implemented artefact. This enables the governing system to govern the enterprise transformation in terms of a clear goal, its current state, and the desired future states of the enterprise. Doing so, implies a perspective on properly governed enterprise transformation as being a form of *engineering*. This gives rise to the field of *enterprise engineering* [28, 14], which is an emerging discipline that regards the design and implementation of enterprises from an *engineering* perspective. Two key paradigms underpin this discipline. The first paradigm states that enterprises are purposefully designed and implemented systems. Consequently, they can be re-designed and re-implemented if there is a need for change. The second paradigm of enterprise engineering is that enterprises are primarily social systems, supported by technical systems. This means that the dominant system elements are social individuals, and that the *essence* of an enterprise's operation lies in the entering into and complying with commitments between these social individuals, while the implementation of this *essence* involves the design of an orchestrated collaboration between social beings and technical artefacts.

In line with [29, 1], the governance of an enterprise transformation process is regarded as involving a force-field between *enterprise strategy*, *programme management* and *enterprise architecture*. When only considering the typical project parameters, one runs the risk of conducting "local optimisations" at the level of specific projects. For example, when making design decisions which have an impact that transcends a specific project, projects will still aim for solutions that provide the best cost/benefits trade-off within the scope of that specific project while not looking at the overall picture. Such local optimisations are likely to damage the overall quality of the result of the transformation [1]. *Enterprise architecture* is concerned with an operationalisation of the direction in which the enterprise aims to transform itself, in terms core properties of the enterprise being engineered. This operationalisation allows the different change projects to be assessed whether they contribute to the realisation of the strategy, while guarding the properties that transcend specific projects.

In this paper we focus on the position of enterprise architecture in relation to enterprise engineering, and the potential roles of principles within this. From that context it is usefull to see architecture as: *the normative restriction of design freedom* [14], allowing enterprise architecture to exert its governing role towards the enterprise transformation. It stresses an important goal of architecture: *to restrict design freedom*, which can also be interpreted as "*to reduce design stress*". This does not exclude architecture as a means for other goals. Indeed [2, 1] classifies architecture viewpoints into *designing*, *deciding*, *contracting* and *informing* viewpoints. Furthermore, in [1] enterprise architecture is positioned explicitly as a means for informed governance of enterprise transformation, requiring indicators and controls to govern enterprise transformations.

The desire to restrict design freedom implies normative instruments with which such restrictions can be made. We believe architecture principles are key instruments in this [30], and we are certainly not alone in doing so. Several approaches position principles as an important ingredient [31, 32, 10, 11, 1, 13, 33, 34], while some even go as far to position principles as being the essence of architecture [14]. Architecture principles fill the gap between high-level strategic intentions and concrete designs. They ensure that the enterprise architecture is future directed, and can actually guide design decisions, while preventing *analysis paralysis* by focussing on the essence. Furthermore, they document fundamental choices in an accessible form, and ease communication with all those affected. They are formulated based on drivers such as strategy, goals and risks. Potential undesired impact on the goals of stakeholders can be reduced by formulating architecture principles.

## 3 A Conceptual Framework for Architecture Principles

As argued before, we take the perspective that architecture principles are a cornerstone of enterprise architecture. The goal of this section, is to provide a conceptual framework for architecture principles. As mentioned before, the framework presented in this paper is the first iteration in a design science [26] driven research effort in which we endeavour to more clearly define the concept of architecture principles, and develop an associated methodology for defining and describing architecture principles. The first iteration as presented in this paper, provides a synthesis of existing views on enterprise architecture and enterprise engineering [27, 1, 14, 13].

### 3.1 History

The term *principle* is said to originate from the Latin word of *principium* [35], which means "origin", "beginning" or "first cause". Vitruvius, an architect in ancient Rome, used principles to explain what is true and indisputable, and should apply to everyone. Vitruvius considered principles as the elements, the laws of nature that produce specific results. For instance, he observed how certain principles of the human body, such as symmetry and proportion, ensure "perfection". The human body was a great source of inspiration to him. He even believed that the principles of the human body should also be applied in the design of gardens and buildings because it would always lead to a perfect result: an ultimate combination of beauty, robustness and usability.

When using principles in the sense of *beginning*, they generally provide insight into the causes of certain effects. These causes can be *laws of nature*, *beliefs* or *rules of conduct. Laws of nature* simply *are*, and influence the things we do. Examples of such principles are the *law of gravity* and the *Pauli exclusion principle*. The latter is a quantum mechanical principle formulated by Wolfgang Pauli in 1925. It states that no two identical fermions may occupy the same quantum state simultaneously. Another example, more directly relevant to enterprise engineering, is the principle of *requisite variety* from general systems theory, which states that a regulating system should match the variety of the system that should be regulated [36].

*Beliefs* are typically founded in moral values. Examples of such principles are Martin Luther King's *principles of nonviolence*, that were to guide the civil rights movement. In an enterprise engineering context, examples of such principles would be: *No wrong doors* (suggesting that clients should be helped at whichever office/desk they approach the enterprise) and *The customer is always right*.

*Rules of conduct* are explicitly defined to influence behaviour, and are typically based on facts and beliefs. General examples include the *Ten Commandments* from the Bible, e.g. *"You shall not murder"* and *"You shall not commit adultery"*. In our enterprise engineering context, examples would be: *Clients can access the entire portfolio of services offered by any part of the government by way of all channels through which government services are offered* and *Before delivering goods and services to external parties, we must hold receipt of the associated payment.*

The remainder of this section will show various dimensions in which principles can be positioned. We distinguish scientific principles from normative principles, positioning architecture principles as normative principles. We divide normative principles into credos and norms, in which the latter form is needed in order to provide enough restriction of design freedom. We show how principles relate to requirements and instructions. Finally, we position architecture as a form of essential design, focusing on the fundamental and essential aspects [37].

## 3.2   Scientific Principles versus Normative Principles

The American Engineers' Council for Professional Development [38] states that engineering concerns *"the creative application of* **scientific principles** *to design or develop structures, machines, apparatus, or manufacturing processes, or works utilising them . . . "*. Principles are used in a wide range of engineering disciplines such as industrial engineering, chemical engineering, civil engineering, electrical engineering and systems engineering. They can be seen as a form of design knowledge that should be shared, in order to increase the quality of designs. In line with [38], we will refer to these principles as *scientific principles*.

*Scientific principles* are likely to be cross-disciplinary in the sense that they will be applicable in various design disciplines. Lidwell [39] provides a list of 100 "universal principles of design", consisting of laws, guidelines, human biases, and general design considerations. The principles can be used as a resource to increase cross-disciplinary knowledge and understanding of design, promote brainstorming and idea generation for design problems, form a checklist of design principles, and to check the quality of design processes and products. Examples of principles described by Lidwell that fall into the category of scientific principles are the *"exposure effect"* and *"performance load"*. The first principle states that *"repeated exposure to stimuli for which people have neutral feelings will increase the likeability of the stimuli"*. The latter states *"the greater the effort to accomplish a task, the less likely the task will be accomplished successfully"*.

Principles have always played an important role in civil engineering, a professional engineering discipline that deals with the design, construction and maintenance of the physical and naturally built environment, including works such as bridges, roads, canals, dams and buildings. Principles from general systems theory, such as the earlier mentioned law of *requisite variety* [36], are examples of scientific principles that are applicable in an enterprise engineering context.

Architecture principles are commonly seen as *normative principles*. TOGAF [13] states that "principles are general rules and guidelines, intended to be enduring and seldom amended, that inform and support the way in which an enterprise sets about fulfilling its mission". The use of principles in the context of enterprise architecture can be traced back to a multi-year deep dive research project led by Michael Hammer, Thomas H. Davenport, and James Champy, called the Partnership for Research in Information Systems Management (or PRISM) [40], which was sponsored by about sixty of the largest global companies (DEC, IBM, Xerox, Texaco, Swissair, Johnson and Johnson, Pacific Bell, AT&T, et cetera). It is a principles based architecture framework, also involving core terminology of, what was at that stage, a novel paradigm. In this context, principles were defined as *"simple, direct statements of an organisation's basic beliefs about how the company wants to use IT in the long term"*. Note that in this definition, the operative word is *wants*. It refers to the fact that fundamentally, such principles are used to express a *normative desire*. Even more, it also expresses how these principles will aim to bridge the communication gap between top management and technical experts. The PRISM model, being from 1986, is among the first published enterprise architecture framework, and as such actually precedes the Zachman framework [41] (published one year later). PRISM's concept of principles as well as how they guide the definition and evolution of architectures was its most salient and widely accepted contribution.

The PRISM model has strongly influenced other enterprise architecture standards, methods and frameworks. The earliest publications referring to the concept of principle, in an enterprise architecture context, can indeed be traced back to the PRISM project [31, 32]. Furhermore, the HP Global Method for IT Strategy and Architecture [34, 42], which is based on work at Digital Equipment Corporation starting in 1984, was almost completely based on the PRISM model and the concept of principles. Many years later, the PRISM report [40] also influenced the IEEE definition of architecture, as many of the IEEE 1471 [27] committee members (Digital included) were employed by the original sponsors of this early work. The concept of *architecture principle* as it is defined in TOGAF [13] today, is also inspired by the PRISM model.

Normative principles do not exist in isolation. They are based on all sorts of other artefacts, such as the strategy, issues, the existing environment and external developments. On the other hand, they also influence all sorts of other artefacts, such as guidelines, requirements, designs and implementations. One can regard the *normative principles* as bridging between strategy and operations; they are primarily an alignment instrument. They are formulated based on knowledge, experience and opinions of all sorts of people in the organisations; senior management, as well as the people that do the actual work. This mixture of people is also the target audience of normative principles. In that sense, the definitions of normative principles also provides a common vocabulary for the organisation.

### 3.3  Credos versus Norms

In practice we see normative principles at various levels of precision. In [24] we have made the distinction between *architecture principles* and *guidelines*, where guidelines are more specific than architecture principles. NORA [43] distinguishes between *fundamental principles* and *derived principles*, where fundamental principles are the basis for derived principles. The level of precision influences the ability to assess the compliance of a design or architecture to the principle. When considering the role of principles bridging between strategy, via architecture to design, this is quite natural. At first, a principle will be formulated rather informally and refined later on in order to use it as a means to restrict design freedom. The definition of the word *principle* in the dictionary [35] suggests multiple forms of principles:

- *1a: a comprehensive and fundamental law, doctrine, or assumption b (1): a rule or code of conduct (2): habitual devotion to right principles <a man of principle> c: the laws or facts of nature underlying the working of an artificial device,*
- *2: a primary source: origin,*
- *3a: an underlying faculty or endowment <such principles of human nature as greed and curiosity> b: an ingredient (as a chemical) that exhibits or imparts a characteristic quality,*
- *4: Christian Science: a divine principle: god.*

In terms of the general definition, *scientific principles* refers to the interpretation of principles as *laws or facts of nature underlying the working of an artificial device*, *normative principles* refers to principles in the sense of a *a comprehensive and fundamental law, doctrine, or assumption* or a *rule of conduct* that guide changes in the enterprises by influencing/directing the design of these changes.

At the start of their life-cycle, normative principles are just statements that express the enterprise's fundamental belief of how things ought to be. At this stage, their exact formulation is less relevant. This is in line with intentions behind TOGAF [13] and the Zachman [41] framework, where the architecture process starts with the creation of an architecture vision. In this phase, architecture is very future-oriented and mostly a creative process. The principles can be used as a means to express a vision, which is mostly based on personal beliefs of the stakeholders involved in the envisioning. They can be seen as normative principles in their initial stage. They are not yet specific enough to actually use them as a norm. In other words; assessing compliance of architectures and designs to these principles is not feasible. They are primarily used as a source of inspiration. Examples of principles in this phase, taken from practical cases, are:

- *We should follow citizen logic.*
- *Work anywhere; anytime.*
- *Reuse as much as possible.*
- *Applications should be decoupled.*

Principles in this phase can best be referred to as being a *credo*. The dictionary [35], defines credo as: "*a set of fundamental beliefs; also: a guiding principle*". This is very close to the definition of principle by Beijer [34]: "*A fundamental approach, belief, or means for achieving a goal...*". In terms of the dictionary definition of principle, we consider this to correspond to its interpretation as *a comprehensive and fundamental law, doctrine, or assumption*. As such, *credos* are things an enterprise consciously chooses to adopt. They represent the fundamental beliefs or assumptions underpinning further architectural decisions. This allows enterprises to provide a first elaboration of an enterprise's strategy towards the desired design of the enterprise.

When enterprises want to use normative principles as a way to actually *limit* design freedom, the principles need to be more specific. This is when the exact formulation of the principle becomes important. They need to be formulated in such a way that compliance to them can be assessed. This starts with a reformulation of the principle statement, but extends to other properties. The full specification will a.o. need to contain definitions of terminology used, as well as a definition of how to assess the compliance of a design to the principle. The examples given previously could be reformulated as follows to make them more specific:

– *The status of customer requests is readily available inside and outside the organization.*
– *All workers are able to work in a time, location and enterprise independent way.*
– *Before buying new application services, it must be clear that such services cannot be rented, and before building such application services ourselves, it must be clear that they can not be purchased.*
– *Communication between application services will take place via an enterprise-wide application service bus.*

Once normative principles have been (re)formulated specific enough to use them to restrict design freedom, we can refer to them as a *norm*. The dictionary [35], defines a norm as: *a principle of right action binding upon the members of a group and serving to guide, control, or regulate proper and acceptable behaviour*. In terms of the dictionary definition of principle, we consider this to correspond to its interpretation as *rule of conduct*. Norms can also be regarded as a tactic by which a *credo* can be enforced. To indeed enable the normative effect of norms, they are required to be *specific, measurable, attainable* and *relevant*.

When considering TOGAF's [13, Section 3.17] definition of principle:

*A qualitative statement of intent that should be met by the architecture. Has at least a supporting rationale and a measure of importance.*

and more specifically the purpose it attributes to such principles [13, Section 36.2.4]:

*Principles are general rules and guidelines, intended to be enduring and seldom amended, that inform and support the way in which an enterprise sets about fulfilling its mission.*

we take the stance that TOGAF requires/presumes architecture principle to be in the form of *norms*.

### 3.4  Principles versus Requirements and Instructions

Normative principles limit design freedom. They are, however, not the only statements which limit design freedom. Requirements also limit design freedom. However, requirements state *what* (functional or constructional) properties a (class of) system(s) should have, and *why* the stakeholders want the (class of) systems to have these properties (also see [34]). Normative principles provide policies on *how* the design of the (class of) system(s) will ensure that the actual implemented system(s) will meet the requirements. Requirements are the basis for solutions, expressing their required characteristics. Fisher [9] states that architecture principles refer to the construction of an enterprise while requirements refer to its function.

Generally, enterprise architectures are not only specified in terms of *normative principles*, but also in terms of more instructive statements, such as models and detailed descriptions on how to apply these in a specific situation. We will refer to these statements as *instructions*, since they tell designers specifically what to do and what not to do. Instructions will refer to the concepts used in the actual construction of the enterprise, such as: value exchanges, transactions, services, contracts, processes, components, objects, building blocks, et cetera. Enterprises typically use languages such as UML [44], BPMN [45], TOGAF's [13] content framework, ArchiMate [3], or the language suggested by the DEMO method [28], to more explicitly express their architectures in terms of concrete modelling concepts. *Instructions*, provide a more operational and tangible refinement of the *normative principles*. Due to their tangible nature, in terms of actual concepts used in the construction of the enterprise, architecture models enable enterprises to study/analyse the effects of different options for the future, as well as analyse problems in the current situation [2]. Just as normative principles, instructions are required to be *specific, measurable, attainable* and *relevant*

Collectively we will refer to *normative principles* and *instructions* as *directives* to express the fact that they both direct the design of the enterprise (albeit at different levels of specificity) and both involve a choice by the enterprise to direct their transformation. The dictionary [35] defines directive as: *serving or intended to guide, govern, or influence*, while the OMG's business motivation model [46] also uses the notion of *directive* as the most general form of guidance/regulation. In terms of the NAF definition of architecture [14], these two flavours of *directive* collectively cover its role as a normative restriction of design freedom.

Figure 1 provides (in the style of Object Role Modelling [47]) a domain model positioning *credos, norms, normative principles, instructions, requirements* and *scientific principles*. In the ORM diagram, the encircled cross is used to signify the fact that *credos, norms, scientific principles, instructions* and *requirements* are mutually exclusive. The general notion of *proposition* is used as a further generalisation of *scientific principles, requirements* and *directives*. Each *proposition* must have a *quality* and a *definition* (signified by the black dot in the diagram), while they have at most one *definition* (signified by the short bar on the fact type).

### 3.5  Architecture Principles versus Design Principles

Regarding an architecture as a *normative restriction of design freedom*, raises the question what the difference is between architecture and design. More operationally, *What*

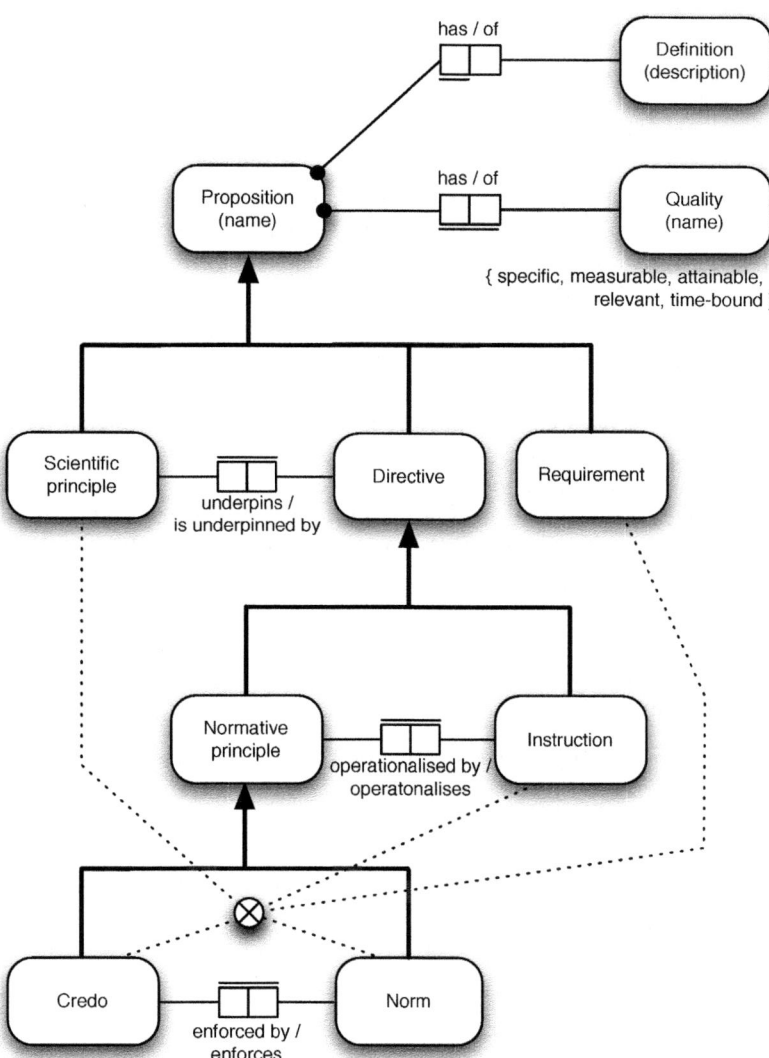

A Credo **must** have Qualities: { attainable, relevant, time-bound }
A Norm **must** have Qualities: { specific, measurable, attainable, relevant, time-bound }
A Instruction **must** have Qualities: { specific, measurable, attainable, relevant, time-bound }
A Scientific principle **must** have Qualities: { specific, measurable }
A Requirement **must** have Qualities: { specific, measurable, attainable, relevant, time-bound }

**Fig. 1.** Core terminology

*should be included in an architecture, and thus restrict the freedom of ensuing design activities, and what should indeed be left to designers?* As suggested by the IEEE [27] and TOGAF [13] definitions of architecture, the architecture level should focus on fundamental aspects. An enterprise architecture should provide an elaboration of an enterprise's strategy, while focussing on the core concerns of the stakeholders. As such, an architecture is typically positioned at a level concerned with a class of systems. A design focuses on the remaining requirements and design decisions pertaining to a specific system being developed, which will typically have a limited impact on the key concerns of the stakeholders.

Fehskens [37] states that architecture should explicitly address alignment, relating the role of architecture to the mission. He redefines architecture as *"those properties of a thing and its environment that are necessary and sufficient for it to be fit for purpose for its mission"*. In his view, architecture should focus on what is essential, on "the stuff that matters". This equates to those properties that are necessary and essential. This is also what distinguishes architecture from design. A different architecture implies a different mission, whilst different designs may address the same mission.

Rivera [42] acknowledges that architecture is about the essense. He adds that generally speaking, design work seeks to find optimal solutions to wellunderstood problems. It's more science than art, algorithmic in nature, and deals mostly with a system's measurable attributes. Architecting deals primarily with nonmeasurable attributes using nonquantitative tools and guidelines based on practical lessons learned. In his view, the architecture uses a heuristic approach. Whereas design and engineering work is primarily deductive in nature, architecture work is primarily inductive.

The distinction between design and architecture, also allows us to distinguish between *architecture* and *design* versions of *normative principles, instructions* and *requirements* respectively:

- *Architecture principles* are normative principles that are included in the architecture of a class of systems.
- *Architecture instructions* are instructions that are included in the architecture of a class of systems.
- *Architecture requirements* are requirements that pertain to the architecture of a class of systems.
- *Design principles* are normative principles included in the design of a specific system.
- *Design instructions* are instructions that are included in the design of a specific system.
- *Design requirements* are requirements that pertain to the design of a specific systems.

The role of these concepts is made even more explicit in Figure 2. In this diagram, concepts from Figure 1 are shown in their architecture and design variants, and guided by scientific principles. The diagram illustrates the flow from strategy via requirements that should already be addressed at the level of the architecture, the actual architecture, the requirements to be met by the design of the system, the design of the system, to the implementation of the system implementation. The scientific principles can be applied during the entire engineering process to motivate design decisions. Note that principles

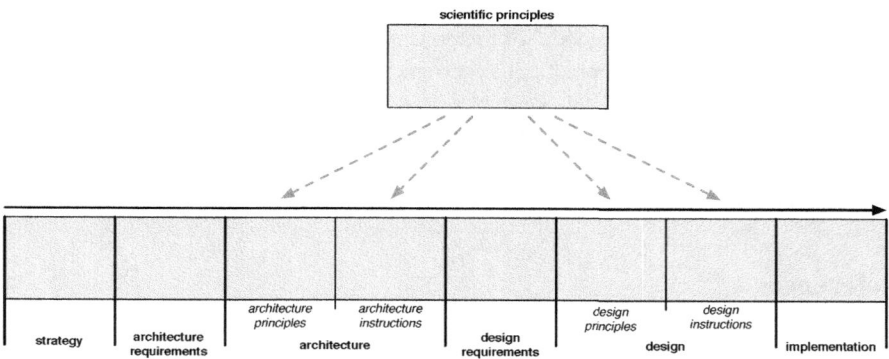

**Fig. 2.** From strategy to implementation

are much less common in designs than in architectures. Rivera [42] even states that "*One of the key differences between the content of descriptions generated from architecture work and that generated from design work is in their use of principles*".

As an illustration of the flow from strategy to implementation, we use a fictitious insurance company. Their strategy is to become the provider of the cheapest insurances in the country. To this end they have formulated the objective to cut costs with 20% within two years, which can be considered an architectural requirement. Based on this requirement they have defined an architecture principle which states that "business processes are standardized and automated". Although they could not find any scientific principles to support this, they had good experiences with process standardization in other organizations. The architecture principle is translated to specific architectural instructions on the claims handling process. These instructions standardize the process by defining the specific activities which must be present in all claims handling processes. A new claims handling system is designed to support the standardized claims handling process. A design requirement for this system is that it integrates with the recently developed customer portal. The lead designer strongly believes that business rules should be defined and implemented separately from other application functionality in this claims handling system and therefore defines the design principle that "business rules are defined in a business rules engine". He also provides more specific design instructions on how to actually define these business rules, by prescribing the specific constructs in the business rules engine that should be used. These design instructions are used by the developers that use the rules engine to implement the system.

## 4   Conclusion

In this paper we have explored the concept of *principle* in relation to enterprise transformations, leading to a conceptual framework more clearly defining *principle* and associated terminology.

The presented framework is the first iteration in a design science [26] driven research effort in which we aim to more clearly define the concept of architecture principles, and develop an associated methodology for defining and describing architecture principles. We have produced a domain model of the concepts involved, taking into account established definitions as well as practical experiences. While the proposed framework is a synthesis of existing theoretical perspectives as well as empirical insights, in line with the design science approach, the necessary next step is to validate this framework in terms of additional practical cases and experiments. With the current conceptual framework in place, we can indeed endeavour to do so.

# References

1. Op't Land, M., Proper, H., Waage, M., Cloo, J., Steghuis, C.: Enterprise Architecture – Creating Value by Informed Governance. Springer, Berlin (2008) ISBN-13: 9783540852315
2. Lankhorst, M., et al.: Enterprise Architecture at Work: Modelling, Communication and Analysis. Springer, Berlin (2005) ISBN-10: 3540243712
3. Iacob, M.E., Jonkers, H., Lankhorst, M., Proper, H.: ArchiMate 1.0 Specification. The Open Group (2009) ISBN-13: 9789087535025
4. Johnson, P., Ekstedt, M.: Enterprise Architecture: Models and Analyses for Information Systems Decision Making. Studentlitteratur (2007) ISBN-13: 9789144027524
5. Iacob, M.E.I., Jonkers, H.: Quantitative analysis of service-oriented architectures. International Journal of Enterprise Information Systems 3, 42–60 (2007)
6. Proper, H., Hoppenbrouwers, S., Veldhuijzen van Zanten, G.: Communication of Enterprise Architectures. In: [2], pp. 67–82, ISBN-10: 3540243712
7. Lankhorst, M., Torre, L.v.d., Proper, H., Arbab, F., Steen, M.: Viewpoints and Visualisation. In: [2], pp. 147–190, ISBN-10: 3540243712
8. Buckl, S., Ernst, A., Lankes, J., Matthes, F.: Enterprise Architecture Management Pattern Catalog - Version 1. Technical Report TB 0801, Technische Universität München, Garching bei München, Germany (2008)
9. Fischer, C., Winter, R., Aier, S.: What is an Enterprise Architecture Design Principle? Towards a consolidated definition. In: Proceedings of the 2nd International Workshop on Enterprise Architecture Challenges and Responses, Yonezawa, Japan (2010)
10. Tapscott, D., Caston, A.: Paradigm Shift – The New Promise of Information Technology. McGraw–Hill, New York (1993) ASIN 0070628572
11. Wagter, R., Berg, M.v.d., Luijpers, J., Steenbergen, M.v.: Dynamic Enterprise Architecture: How to Make It Work. Wiley, New York (2005) ISBN-10: 0471682721
12. Capgemini: Enterprise, Business and IT Architecture and the Integrated Architecture Framework. White paper, Utrecht, The Netherlands (2007)
13. The Open Group – TOGAF Version 9. Van Haren Publishing, Zaltbommel, The Netherlands (2009) ISBN-13: 9789087532307
14. Dietz, J.: Architecture – Building strategy into design. Netherlands Architecture Forum. Academic Service – SDU, The Hague (2008), http://www.naf.nl ISBN-13: 9789012580861
15. Lindström, Å.: On the Syntax and Semantics of Architectural Principles. In: Proceedings of the 39th Hawaii International Conference on System Sciences (2006)
16. Lindström, Å.: An Approach for Developing Enterprise-Specific ICT Management Methods – From Architectural Principles to Measures. In: IAMOT 2006 – 15th International Conference on Management of Technology, Beijing, China (2006)
17. Lee, C.: Aerospace Logistics architecture program: Action Research at Air France Cargo – KLM Cargo. Master's thesis, Delft Technical University, Delft, The Netherlands (2006)

18. Go, A.: Implementing Enterprise Architecture: Action Research at Air France Carge – KLM Cargo. Master's thesis, Delft Technical University, Delft, The Netherlands (2006)
19. Kersten, J.: Propositions. Master's thesis, Radboud University Nijmegen, Nijmegen, The Netherlands (2009) (in Dutch)
20. Boekel, K.v.: Architectuurprincipes: Functie en Formulering (Architecture Principles: Function and Formulation. Master's thesis, Radboud University Nijmegen, Nijmegen, The Netherlands (2009) (in Dutch)
21. Tillaart, M.v.d.: Propositions into a Framework. Master's thesis, Radboud University Nijmegen, Nijmegen, The Netherlands (2009)
22. Ramspeck, B.: Formulating Principles in an Effective Way. Master's thesis, Radboud University Nijmegen, Nijmegen, The Netherlands (2008)
23. Greefhorst, D., Proper, H., Ham, F.v.d.: Principes: de hoeksteen voor architectuur – Verslag van een workshop op het Landelijk Architectuur Congres 2007 (Principles: The Cornerstone of Architecture – A report of a workshop held at the Dutch National Architecture Congres 2007. Via Nova Architectura (2007) (in Dutch), http://www.via-nova-architectura.org
24. Greefhorst, D.: ICT bibliotheek. In: Ervaringen met het opstellen van architectuurprincipes bij een verzekeraar (Experiences with the formulation of architecture principles at an insurance company), vol. 35, ch. 2, pp. 53–62. Academic Service – SDU, The Hague (2007) (in Dutch) ISBN-13: 9789012119511
25. Bouwens, S.: DYA Architectuurprincipes – Deel 1: Basics (DYA Architecture Principles – Part 1: Basics). White paper, Sogeti, The Netherlands (2008) (in Dutch )
26. Hevner, A., March, S., Park, J., Ram, S.: Design Science in Information Systems Research. MIS Quarterly 28, 75–106 (2004)
27. The Architecture Working Group of the Software Engineering Committee, Standards Department, IEEE: Recommended Practice for Architectural Description of Software Intensive Systems. Technical Report IEEE P1471:2000, ISO/IEC 42010:2007, The Architecture Working Group of the Software Engineering Committee, Standards Department, IEEE, Piscataway, New Jersey (2000) ISBN-10: 0738125180
28. Dietz, J.: Enterprise Ontology – Theory and Methodology. Springer, Berlin (2006) ISBN-10: 9783540291695
29. Rijsenbrij, D., Schekkerman, J., Hendrickx, H.: Architectuur, besturingsinstrument voor adaptieve organisaties – De rol van architectuur in het besluitvormingsproces en de vormgeving van de informatievoorziening, Lemma, Utrecht, The Netherlands (2002) (in Dutch) ISBN-10: 9059310934
30. Op't Land, M., Proper, H.: Impact of Principles on Enterprise Engineering. In: Österle, H., Schelp, J., Winter, R. (eds.) Proceedings of the 15th European Conference on Information Systems, University of St. Gallen, St. Gallen, Switzerland, pp. 1965–1976 (2007)
31. Davenport, T., Hammer, M., Metsisto, T.: How executives can shape their company's information systems. Harvard Business Review 67, 130–134 (1989)
32. Richardson, G., Jackson, B., Dickson, G.: A Principles-Based Enterprise Architecture: Lessons from Texaco and Star Enterprise. MIS Quarterly 14, 385–403 (1990), http://www.jstor.org/stable/249787
33. Hartman, H., Hofman, A., Stahlecker, M., Waage, M., Wout, J.v.h.: The Integrated Architecture Framework Explained. Springer, Berlin (2010) ISBN-13: 9783642115172
34. Beijer, P., de Klerk, T.: IT Architecture: Essential Practice for IT Business Solutions. Lulu (2010)
35. Meriam–Webster: Meriam–Webster Online, Collegiate Dictionary (2003)
36. Beer, S.: Diagnosing the System for Organizations. Wiley, New York (1985)
37. Fehskens, L.: Re-Thinking architecture. In: 20th Enterprise Architecture Practitioners Conference, The Open Group (2008)

38. The Engineers' Council for Professional Development. Science 94, 456 (1941)
39. Lidwell, W., Holden, K., Butler, J.: Universal Principles of Design. Rockport Publishers, Inc., Massachusetts (2003)
40. CSC Index, Inc., Hammer & Company, Inc., Cambridge MA.: PRISM: Dispersion and Interconnection: Approaches to Distributed Systems Architecture, Final Report. Technical report, CSC Index, Inc. and Hammer & Company, Inc. Cambridge, MA (1986)
41. Zachman, J.: A framework for information systems architecture. IBM Systems Journal 26 (1987)
42. Rivera, R.: Am I Doing Architecture or Design Work? It Professional 9, 46–48 (2007)
43. ICTU: Nederlandse Overheid Referentie Architectuur 2.0 – Samenhang en samenwerking binnen de elektronische overheid (2007) (in Dutch), http://www.ictu.nl
44. OMG: UML 2.0 Superstructure Specification – Final Adopted Specification. Technical Report ptc/03–08–02, OMG (2003)
45. Object Management Group: Business process modeling notation, v1.1. OMG Available Specification OMG Document Number: formal/2008-01-17, Object Management Group (2008)
46. BMM Team: Business Motivation Model (BMM) Specification. Technical Report dtc/06–08–03, Object Management Group, Needham, Massachusetts (2006)
47. Halpin, T., Morgan, T.: Information Modeling and Relational Databases, 2nd edn. Data Management Systems. Morgan Kaufman, San Francisco (2008) ISBN-13: 9780123735683

# Leveraging Software Architectures through the ISO/IEC 42010 Standard: A Feasibility Study

Damien A. Tamburri[1,2], Patricia Lago[1], and Henry Muccini[2]

[1] VU University Amsterdam, The Netherlands
[2] Università dell'Aquila, Italy

**Abstract.** The state of the practice in enterprise and software architecture learnt that relevant architectural aspects should be illustrated in multiple views, targeting the various concerns of different stakeholders. This has been expressed a.o. in the ISO/IEC 42010 Standard on architecture descriptions. In the same vein, the research community observed that Architecture Description Languages, or ADLs, should be developed to address stakeholders' concerns concentrating on the use of viewpoints for their description. This notwithstanding, we notice today a proliferation of ADLs impervious to these guidelines. This imperviousness creates a gap between what the IT industry requires and what ADLs can provide. This gap makes it impossible for practitioners to choose and use the best-fit ADL for his/her requirements. To fill this gap, we must analyze the existing ADLs, and mine and make explicit their addressed concerns, views, viewpoints, and stakeholders. Such an explicit overview can provide practitioners with pragmatic information for selecting the most suitable ADL, and hence support them in the architecting process. This paper reports on initial results in this direction. Given a specific ADL (namely, DARWIN/FSP), it presents a feasibility study on the methodology mapping the concepts of the ISO/IEC 42010 on the DARWIN/FSP ADL.

**Keywords:** Software Architecture, ADLs, Enterprise Architecture, Architecture Viewpoints, Architecture Views.

## 1 Introduction

A large number of ADLs [22] from the academic community exists, but still finds localized consensus from the mainstream IT market. Our goal is that of analyzing both the types of needs of IT practitioners as represented by the ISO/IEC 42010 standard for architecture description [5], and the potentials of ADLs to fulfill such needs. We argue that bridging this gap is the key step to: *(a)* render ADLs an industrial asset in IT enterprises; *(b)* enable IT practitioners to choose a "best fit" ADL; *(c)* ease the description of software architectures in IT enterprises by means of ADLs for modeling [9], and of views/viewpoints for expressing all needed information as a taxonomical map [10]. Our contribution to this goal is a method to map standard elements from ISO/IEC 42010 on a certain ADL. We chose a case study driven approach gathering feasibility data from experience.

E. Proper et al. (Eds.): TEAR 2010, LNBIP 70, pp. 71–85, 2010.

Since we needed an ADL that outlived others in order to evaluate the impact over time of the standard, the ADL we chose is DARWIN/FSP, given its long-lived career as an architecture description technology.

We argue that the contribution of the method we explored is in its potential to assess ADLs' fitness in leveraging information to the enterprise architecture level, adapting it to various types of stakeholders by means of multiple views. Thanks to our methodology, ADLs and their views could be proven fit in managing information within the IT, too, since alignment between information artifacts in enterprise architectures is of extreme importance [27] in its own.

The paper is structured as follows: in Section 2 we show an introduction to the two main technologies involved in this study, namely ISO/IEC 42010 Recommended practice for architectural description of software-intensive systems [5] and DARWIN/FSP. Section 3 explains our main goal by stating the problem that moved this research in the first place, while in Section 4 we expose our research questions. Section 5 delivers the methodology we followed to analyze the primary papers and the meta-model for DARWIN/FSP. Finally, Section 6 illustrates the results achieved in the study, while Section 7 concludes the paper.

## 2    Background Introduction

This section will introduce briefly the two main technologies involved in this study as a reference to the rest of the paper, namely DARWIN/FSP [14] and ISO/IEC 42010 [5].

DARWIN was developed in the early 90's at Imperial College as an architectural description language which would tackle the unknown frontiers of architectural modeling and analysis, a rather unexplored topic at the time. To this aim the authors tried to solve a number of architectural reasoning strongpoints by providing a modeling notation and its analysis counterpart: DARWIN and FSP. DARWIN is by definition of the authors [14], [15] a well-structured, declarative configuration language, i.e. a description language which enables the formal specification of composable software architecture structures. These structures are de-composable (i.e. with sub-elements) and constraints may be deployed on the design for it to uphold and maintain certain architectural properties or style constraints. FSP is a labelled-transition system like notation which enables proper modeling of system behavior in the form of composable and parallelizable finite state authms; this design is possibly fed to LTSA [13], an LTS analyzer which is able in turn to check properties on the behavioral specification. The metamodel for the technology can be found in [21].

Quoting [5], the ISO/IEC 42010 standard's chief aim is that of addressing " *[..] the creation, analysis and sustainment of architectures of systems through the use of architecture descriptions. A conceptual model of architecture description is established.*". The elements in the standard's core meta-model are so defined:

– *system of interest:* system whose architecture is under consideration and is the subject of an architecture description.

- *stakeholder:* individual, team, organization, or classes thereof, having concerns with respect to a system.
- *system concern:* interest in a system important to one or more of its stakeholders.
- *architecture viewpoint:* work product establishing the conventions for the construction, interpretation and use of architecture views.
- *model kind:* conventions for one type of modeling.
- *architecture model:* a discrete part of an architecture view consisting of architecture description elements.
- *architecture view:* work product expressing the architecture of a system from the perspective of system concerns.
- *architecture rationale:* explanation or justification for architecture decisions.
- *architecture description:* work product used to express an architecture.
- *architecture:* fundamental concepts or properties of a system in its environment embodied in elements, relationships, and principles of its design and evolution.

Additional elements we considered have been taken from the other meta-models in the standard. For the sake of space we do not treat them here, but refer the reader to [5].

## 3   Problem Statement

As defined in [5], stakeholder concerns expressed by industrial parties can be seen as properties to be upkept by the architecture. In the same vein, an architecture can be illustrated in views [24,18,4]. Since views are conforming to viewpoints [26,4], and ADL-driven views are conforming to ADL definitions (via the "meta-model <=> model" relation [8]), we argue that by mapping ADLs (and their promised properties) on the 42010 standard (and its stakeholder concerns) [5] we offer a natural mechanism to ensure that resulting software architecture models will also yield the desired properties. Moreover we argue that with this mechanism and the kind of information it provides, we offer a map to guide practitioners towards the assessment of ADLs, ultimately to choose the "best fit" ADL for their purposes.

## 4   Research Questions

Given the problem at hand, our main research question can be formulated as follows: *how can we map 42010 concepts on ADL concepts, so as to map ADL properties onto viewpoints' concerns while obtaining pragmatic information on the ADL itself?*

By giving an answer to this question we provide the means for an IT enterprise to choose an ADL by stating its desired properties or additionally, by seeing which properties can be expressed by which ADL and in which view, addressing which concerns, and so on.

There are many possible ways to answer our main research question. One possible way is modeling an industrial success story (i.e. a successful industrial application of concepts such as software architecture, viewpoints etc.) with the ADL and checking if it fully complies with ISO/IEC 42010. Another way might be to consider success stories previously modeled in the ADL and map elements contained there, on the concepts from the standard. In loose line with this second approach, we chose to carry out a case study with the general structure described in Figure 1. The ADL at hand was investigated both in its meta-model and its publications.

Our main research question has been refined into the following questions:

1. *what are the concepts from ISO/IEC 42010 to be used in the mapping?*
   In order to use the standard as a map on ADLs it must be analyzed and its elements must be pruned according to study requirements. The set of concepts to be used in the mapping have to be defined. In addition, the elements on which these concepts were to be mapped on the ADL had to be defined as well.

2. *how do we map the extracted concepts from ISO/IEC 42010 on a certain ADL?*
   The way in which the concepts from the standard may be mapped onto a certain ADL must be chosen. We used an exhaustive word and relations search for our primary studies and a search for instances of the concepts expressed in the standard for the meta-model. Relations from the standard were also investigated on the meta-model.

## 5   The Case Study: Design

Keeping in mind the research statement we exposed in Section 3 and using our research questions as guidelines we designed our study as follows.

As shown in Figure 1, the process we adopted is a top-down approach; by means of it we can obtain a set of ISO/IEC compliance Tables, for a certain ADL. These Tables carry the pragmatic information we were looking for, as introduced in Section 1. We initiated our study by selecting primary study papers to consider for the DARWIN/FSP ADL (branch 1a in Figure 1). We procured primary studies from an initial pool of four publications we previously investigated in previous work [21]. We merged these results with the ones obtained through a on-line search[1] following standard guidelines for systematic literature search. For our search, inclusion criteria have been: (*i*) direct research or work on the selected ADL; (*ii*) treatment of essential parts or implications of the selected ADL; (*iii*) enhancement to the technological core of the selected ADL. Exclusion criteria have been: (*i*) unrelated or loosely related publications (i.e. publications that had only minor reference to the ADL in object or merely cited the ADL itself for "related work" purposes); (*ii*) success stories, as they use the technology rather than describing it; (*iii*) research works enhancing the ADL.

---

[1] Google-scholar, google, ACM digital library, DBLP.

With this approach, a total of 9 primary studies [17,19,11,16,15,14,6,13,7] of various nature in addition to Kramer and Magee's book [12] were selected.

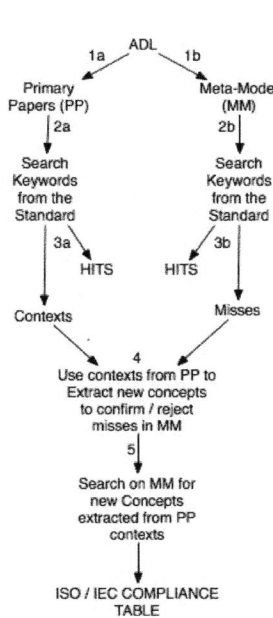

Further on, we obtained a meta-model of DAR-WIN/FSP from previous research efforts [21] (branch 1b in Figure 1). We then extracted the full extent of keywords available in ISO/IEC 42010 and captured them on a Table representing: *(a)* the keywords themselves; *(b)* the keywords' synonyms; *(c)* the terms each keyword is related with. For sake of space the table is only available online[2].

Synonyms in the query table were obtained by searching every keyword in Google's On-Line Dictionary[3]. Relations amongst terms are taken directly from conceptual meta-models in Figures 1 to 5 from [5]. Columns marked in grey (in all Tables) identify all the new elements that were added in the ISO/IEC 42010 as compared to the older standard IEEE 1471 for architecture description [20].

With the Query Table at hand, we exhaustively searched all keywords both on the papers and on the DARWIN/FSP meta-model (branch 2a and 2b in Figure 1): on the papers with the "advanced-search" option within Adobe Professional 6.0 and by direct comparison of the DARWIN/FSP and ISO/IEC 42010 complete meta-models. We searched keywords first, then all synonyms.

**Fig. 1.** Analysis process structure

We initially looked up the keywords and their synonyms and reported HIT or MISS (branch 3a in Figure 1). Contextual information from the papers (i.e. the context in which the word was found on the primary study) for each HIT was then captured in brackets.

We then compared results from the paper investigation with the meta-model look-up, to mutually confirm results.

Misses in the papers and the meta-model were handled in the following way: *(i)* If a MISS was found on the papers, then we verified if the word was composite (e.g. software architecture = software + architecture); if it was, an additional search was made with the "main part" of the composite word (i.e. the part that pertains the most with the study itself: e.g. software architecture ==> search for "architecture"). If an additional MISS was found then a MISS was accepted and the space in the results Table was left blank. Because it is common for publications to report composite terms only in their key parts (e.g. software architecture ==> architecture).

---

[2] http://docs.google.com/Doc?docid=0AQzadZCY_
NCHZGN0N2pzbmRfMjJmOGNmNnA5dw&hl=en
[3] http://www.google.com/dictionary

*(ii)* if a MISS was found on the meta-model, then we have two cases: *(1)* the same keyword MISS was present on the paper side, in this case, MISS was accepted as such; *(2)* a HIT for the same keyword was present on the paper side. In this second case, the context from the HIT was used to extract concepts (branch 4 of Figure 1) to be searched again on the meta-model (branch 5 of Figure 1); this to double-check the results. If a miss was found again, then it was accepted as such.

Table 1 was resulting from the investigation on the papers: the list of publications is ordered by increasing publication year. Note that main keywords were written in normal text on the Table whereas synonyms are written in italic. Table 3 recaps results from the investigation of the meta-model. Besides the keywords on the standard, we also analyzed the relations between them. Results for this are captured in Table 2 for the papers and Table 3 for the meta-model. This last investigation is relevant to analyze keywords also via their relations found and where: indeed many of the findings which refer to two or more words found on the papers, are concluded by analyzing results from Table 1 and double checking them with results from Table 2. Also, many inconsistencies between concepts' relations in ISO/IEC 42010 and the DARWIN/FSP meta- model can be pointed out by analyzing results from this investigation.

To generate Table 2, we inspected Table 1, since each relation only exists if both elements (in the relation) exist in the same publication. Therefore, for every relation between keywords we verified the logical "AND" of each relation directly on Table 1: "HIT1 *logic_ and* HIT2", where HIT1 and HIT2 are the investigation results (contained in Table 1). Each cell in Table 2 contains the publication where a relation is found between the column and row keywords (HIT1 and HIT2 respectively).

In more formal terms, this Table is an "N * N" matrix where N is the number of elements from the standard. The (n*m)-th cell contains the publications that have both the "n"-th and the "m"-th term.

Results from this Table act as a semantical blueprint for the keywords for two main reasons: *(a)* it provides data on where the keywords that refer to others are present; *(b)* shows how keyword relations (i.e. the meaning and implications of keywords) are present and to which depth for the ADL.

Given the limited size of both the meta-models at hand, we compared them in Table 3. For the meta-models, we looked for instances of the classes represented by the standard keywords (e.g. for the "Architecture Description" keyword we searched for artifacts which represented a DARWIN architecture description, and we found the "DarwinSpecification" element which was significant). The standard itself becomes a map for the ADL meta-model, i.e. a reference meta-meta-model [25]. So the methodology for finding relations on the meta-model became: *(i)* take all the elements from the standard; *(ii)* using them as meta-concepts, search on the meta-model instances of them or concepts semantically close (i.e. which essentially express the same meaning); *(iii)* take all relations from the standard; *(iv)* check if the same relations are held between the concepts found; *(v)* capture results.

Additionally, automated methodologies for comparing and differencing models (and therefore meta-models) are also present in research [3,1,23]. Analysis results are discussed in the next Section.

## 6   The Case Study: Execution Results

This section explains the results of our study, as summarized in Tables 1 and 2 for the primary studies, and in Table 3 for the meta-model. In all Tables, blank spaces represent misses. Analyzing these Tables led to the following observations:

- Consider results in **Table 1**. When investigating "architecture rationale" as such (column 14) it is evident that there is little to no direct reference to "rationale"'s, not in views, nor in viewpoints nor in architectural decisions and reasoning practices; there is also an evident lack of formality when it comes to architectural reasoning practices and definitions.
- By looking at the publication date of the primary studies, and at terms "architecture rationale" (column 14) and "correspondence rule" (column 7): the further back in time we go, the less common become keywords from the 42010 standard (as compared to synonyms or decomposed words). This suggests that standard notations provided a fair degree of consensus, as further confirmed when we explored the documentation.
- Consider terms "architecture rationale" (column 14) and "stakeholder" (column 3): entries are almost completely missing. Indeed, stakeholders and all the implications thereto are scarcely considered. If reasoning on them is allowed or supported, there is little or no exploration of domain- and stakeholder concerns which might be behind properties being verified. Specifically, "stakeholder" itself is never found on the primary studies except once and in the form of synonym ("decision maker"). This means that focus on stakeholder concerns is still very limited if present at all. This hinders dramatically the success rate of ADL industrial adoption as this technology is still unable to properly express the concerns important for enterprises.
- Consider "view" and "viewpoint" (columns 9 and 12) from Table 1 and for each HIT, consider the context in braces: in older papers, the definition of standard viewpoints is missing. More in general, there are indeed big inconsistencies between view and viewpoint definitions across the papers. This means that ADLs do not provide a focused vision on what description they realize and how. Resulting descriptions are mixed, misaligned and ultimately confusing.
- Further on "view" and "viewpoint" (columns 9 and 12): correspondence between the seemingly complementary views in DARWIN is overlooked, since a match between HITs of the former and the latter cannot be done given the context in brackets. Therefore, no direct definition of the complementary nature intended for the two vistas is present. Moreover from columns "model correspondence" and "correspondence rule" (columns 6 and 7) it is evident that correspondence between instances in the two views is loose and no direct model correspondence can be identified precisely anywhere in the

primary studies. Again this point confirms that ADLs provide misaligned views. Since alignment is critical in enterprises, ADLs may result hostile.

- In general, if we consider all the greyed columns in Table 1: all these elements have been covered in current publications quite loosely, if at all. The standard is calling here for standardization of 'new' concepts that still need to be introduced in the architecture description community. This means that ADLs are outdated, careless of standard practices and still too far from effective enterprise needs.
- Consider now the absence of HITs for term "framework" (column 8); this identifies a lack of cohesion in the ADL at hand. This notion indicates therefore that this ADL in particular lacks the idea of a basic conceptual structure used to solve or reason about complex architectural issues. This notion underlines the need for more clarity and conceptual background for ADLs.
- As for term "system of interest" (column 1): we found there is absolutely no mention of system of interest. The selected ADL strongly points at concurrent systems and makes no reference to additional potential usage. No exploration effort whatsoever, was ever poured into this direction. This means that ADLs are un-targeted, consider no focused direction and ultimately try to reach a scope of systems too broad for it to be meaningful.
- When filling column 13 for term "model kind", it became evident to us that there are typed elements but no model typing. Rather, models have exposition targets (i.e. Software Architecture details they must capture). Moreover, typing of models and reasoning about model kinds is only found at a formal and semantic level in the most recent of our primary study, DARWIN/FSP language BNF, and therefore outside of the specific architecture description domain. This means that still there is a lack of concepts in the ADL. Further, ADLs are too distant from the Model Driven trends that are evident now in enterprise architecture.
- When filling column 10 "architecture decision", we found out that there is no direct mention of decisions, rather of properties to be checked on diagrams. It is noticeable also that "architecture decision" finds HITs only in older publications. This means that newer works do not focus on capturing architectural design decisions either, hence neglecting the recognized shift of architecture to a set of design decisions [2].
- By cross checking **Table 2** with results in Table 1 it can be noticed that there is little or no "direct" relation verification, meaning that relations are seldom verified with HITs of main keywords from the standard. Most relations are in fact verified thanks to synonyms of related terms. This means that there is little compliance between DARWIN/FSP, with the guidelines used in ISO/IEC 42010. Indeed ADLs are far from the concepts needed in the IT world and the standard provides a valuable recollection of such concepts.
- There are only a few publications which carry a significant amount of HITs, i.e. lots of terms and relations are hit/verified in a limited amount of publications. Moreover, overviewing Table 2, it is apparent that a very limited amount of relations are verified; this identifies a serious lack of concern for the implications and influences each term has with other concepts.

- Carefully analyze Table 2 as a whole: either relations are present/treated in different (i.e. more than one) publications or they are not present at all. This can either mean clear distinction of boundaries of the application domain for DARWIN/FSP or a formally specified technology with a rather strict focus of the technology itself.
- Check on Table 2 all the entries that are marked in grey. Again these entries identify the new elements w.r.t. the older IEEE 1471 standard for architecture description. Relations for the new elements are scarce. This again provides proof that ADLs are still inconsistent with agreed upon standards and terminologies.
- Checking Table 2 it becomes evident that important terms' relations such as "architecture rationale", "model kind", "architecture decision" and even "software architecture" itself are unexplored, loosely considered and ultimately left for open interpretation. This point provides evidence that there is still a strong need for more clarity of concerns for ADLs. ADLs need to relax their targeted front of systems.
- From data on Table 2 and given what was stated earlier concerning "views" and "viewpoints" in DARWIN/FSP, one would expect the relations involving "view" and "viewpoint" to be loosely present. Indeed these two terms carry many results, which identifies the author's will to sustain the existence of a relation between the two keywords, but the concepts behind them are only loosely implemented and evident on the primary studies (as evident from Table 1). This means that ADLs do recognize the need for the separation of concerns into views and viewpoints but at the same time do fail in implementing this division. The technology is too rooted around the legacy concepts that originally moved it.

Following on, these findings were made while inspecting the meta-model results **Table 3**:

- Consider the elements added in ISO/IEC 42010 (grey columns): inspection of the meta-model confirmed DARWIN/FSP's lack of new and fundamental concepts present in the standard, and hence needed in modern IT software ecosystems. Moreover, consider the two columns with HITS, "archi. decision" and "model kind": it seems that while decisions made at an architectural level may be expressed as constants and constraints but the rationale behind them is left away.
- Consider elements "model correspondence" and "correspondence rule": the absence of these two terms at the meta-model level reveals a deep shortfall within its structure. The mapping between the architecture in DARWIN and its behavior in FSP is reported on the meta-model with a simple association and has no additional specification. This means that the two separate blueprints of the system are merely juxtaposed and linked rather than intermingled. This strongly enforces our hypotheses made by inspecting Tables 1 and 2.

**Table 1.** Results after applying the first branch of the mapping strategy

| Element / Terms | 1) Sys. of interest | 2) software architecture | 3) stake-holder | 4) concern | 5) architecture description | 6) model corresp. | 7) corresp. rule | 8) framework | 9) arch. viewpoint | 10) arch. decision | 11) arch. model | 12) arch. view | 13) Model Kind | 14) architecture rationale |
|---|---|---|---|---|---|---|---|---|---|---|---|---|---|---|
| [16], '95 | | | | HIT: concern (dynamism of SAs and structural concerns) | | HIT: correspondence (correspondences between compo. & interf.) | | | | | | HIT: view (representation and devel. of models) | | |
| [16], '95 | | HIT: SA (state of the art, integration of views) | | | HIT: structural description (Software architect's modeling efforts) | | HIT: rules (program devel.: forward engin.) | | | HIT: decision (SA reasoning) | HIT: model (behavior verification) | HIT: SA view (SA analysis, view integrat., config. view) | | HIT: design rationale (user defined attribs.) |
| [14], '95 | | HIT: archi-tecture, design, (system de-velopment) | | HIT: concern (distributed systems' de-velopment) | HIT: description (structural definition) | HIT: model conformance (model flexibil.) | | | | | | | | |
| [7], '97 | | HIT: design (system V&V) | HIT: decision maker (system V&V) | HIT: concern (concur-rency) | HIT: repre-sentation (multiple concurrency rep.) | | | | | | HIT: model, pattern, repres. (architecture specifica-tion) | HIT: view (concur-rency descrip-tion) | | |
| [11], '99 | | | | | HIT: description (architecture structural description) | | | | HIT: point of view (system description, deadlock prevention); HIT: viewpoint (developing the system architec-ture) | HIT: decision (design, type params) | HIT: model, pattern (concurrency verification and description) | | | HIT: arch. practice (architecture assumption) |
| [6], '99 | HIT: softw. system design (system design and verif.) | HIT: archi-tecture, design (system behavior modeling + V&V) | | HIT: concern, interest (system QoS, verification of properties) | HIT: description, representa-tion (Architecture specification) | | HIT: rule (compo-nent instances) | | HIT: point of view (behavioral and architec-tural) | | | HIT: view, (structure and behav. modeling) | HIT: form, kind (LTL mod. check.) | HIT: practice (describing and evaluating system properties) |
| [13], '99 | | HIT: softw. architecture (behavior spec. & analysis) | | | HIT: SA desc. (behav. modelling and verif.) | | | | HIT: aspect (SA behavior specs.) | | HIT: model (SA descriptive artifact, Behavior description, behavior analysis) | HIT: view (LTS view of a sys.'s behavior) | | |
| [17], '03 | | HIT: architecture (system design and verification) | | | HIT: architecture description (systems verification) | | | | | | HIT: model (architecture verification, future work) | HIT: view, vision, (multiple view support) | | |
| [19], '04 | HIT: software system (proper behav.+ arch. descript.) | HIT: archi-tecture, structure, skeleton (lack of a proper SA definition) | | | HIT: architectural description (ADLs and ADL definition) | | | | HIT: viewpoint (related efforts) | | | HIT: view (syntax of DARWIN, ADL grammar) | HIT: kind (static /dyn. model type) | |
| [12], '06 | | | | | | | HIT: inference rules (grammar definition) | | | | | | HIT: type (BNF def.) | |

**Table 2.** Results of the search for relationships amongst terms

| Terms / Terms | system of interest | architecture | stakeholder | concern | architecture description | model correspondence | corresp. rule | framework | viewpoint | architectural decision | architectural model | view | model kind | rationale |
|---|---|---|---|---|---|---|---|---|---|---|---|---|---|---|
| system of interest | | | | | | | | | | | | | | |
| architecture | [6] | | | | | | | | | | | | | |
| stakeholder | | | | [7] | [7] | | | | [7] | | | | | |
| concern | | | [7] | | [7], [6], [14] | | | | [7], [6] | | | | | |
| arch. description | | [6], [17], [19], [15], [14], [7], [13] | [7] | [7], [14], [6] | | [15] | | | [19], [11], [13], [7], [6] | | | [6], [15], [13], [17], [7], [19] | | [11], [15], [6] |
| model correspond. | | | | | [15] | | | | | | | | | |
| correspondence rule | | | | | | [15] | | | | | | | | |
| framework | | | | | | | | | | | | | | |
| viewpoint | | | [7] | [7], [6] | [7], [6], [13], [19] | | | | | | [7], [13] | [7], [19], [13], [6] | [6], [19] | |
| architectural decision | | | | | | | | | | | | | [12] | |
| arch. model | | | | | [7], [6], [13], [19], [15], [17] | [15] | | | [7], [13] | | | [7], [15], [13], [17] | | |
| view | | | | | | | | | [7], [6], [13], [19] | [11], [15] | [7], [15], [13], [17] | | | |
| model kind | | | | | | | | | | | | | | |
| rationale | | | | | [15], [11], [6] | | | | | | | | | |

**Table 3.** Results of the meta-model look up of standard terms and relations

| Element in DARWIN/FSP | 1) Sys. of interest | 2) software architecture | 3) stake-holder | 4) system concern | 5) architecture description | 6) model corresp. | 7) corresp. rule | 8) frame-work | 9) architecture viewpoint | 10) arch. decision | 11) architecture model | 12) arch. view | 13) Model Kind | 14) arch. rationale |
|---|---|---|---|---|---|---|---|---|---|---|---|---|---|---|
| DARWIN | | | | ? - HIT: Constant Declaration - ? | HIT: DarwinSpecification | | | | ? - HIT: DarwinSpecification - ? | HIT: Constant Declaration | ? - HIT: DarwinSpecification - ? | | ? - HIT: Darwin Specification - ? | |
| FSP | | | | ? - HIT: Constant - ? | HIT: FspSpecification | | | | ? - HIT: FspSpecification - ? | HIT: Constant | ? - HIT: FspSpecification - ? | | ? - HIT: FspSpecification - ? | |

| Terms / Terms | system of interest | architecture | stake-holder | arch. concern | arch. descript. | model correspondence | corresp. rule | framework | arch. viewpoint | arch. decision | model | arch. view | model kind | rationale |
|---|---|---|---|---|---|---|---|---|---|---|---|---|---|---|
| system of interest | | | | | | | | | | | | | | |
| architecture | | | | | | | | | | | | | | |
| stakeholder | | | | | | | | | | | | | | |
| arch. concern | | | | | X | | | | | X | | | | |
| description | | | | X | | | | | X | | X | | X | |
| model correspond. | | | | | | | | | | | | | | |
| corresp. rule | | | | | | | | | | | | | | |
| framework | | | | | X | | | | X | | | | | |
| arch. viewpoint | | | | | | | | | | X | X | | X | |
| arch. decision | | | | X | X | | | | X | | | | X | |
| arch. model | | | | | | | | | | | | | | |
| arch. view | | | | | | | | | | | | | | |
| model kind | | | | | X | | | | X | | X | | | |
| rationale | | | | | | | | | | | | | | |

- On Table 3 the presence of instances for "architecture decision" in the meta-model enforces our hypothesis that decisions can be realized with constants and constraints but these cannot be traced to entities representing the concerns and decisions that brought them about. This means that potential adopters will find it difficult to keep architectural data consistent and meaningful.
- Again on Table 3, It is indeed noticeable that within dozens of elements within the meta- model merely two can be instances of elements from the standard. Therefore, the meta-model has no sufficient power as to express its potential properly, abstract classes such as "software architecture" or "architecture element" in it are missing. These might have been used to match them with additional keywords such as "software architecture" from the standard.
- Consider relations: no relations exist between the concept of "view" and the concept of "viewpoint" hence confirming our inconsistency of concepts hypothesis. Indeed the two concepts are misinterpreted and ultimately misused.
- Consider again relations: the absence of relations between the new keywords introduced in ISO/IEC 42010. One would expect that a proper meta-model exhibited some of these relations even if no mention was made in the primary studies, as these relations ensure the correct behavior and power of expression of the meta-model itself. On the contrary these relations are missing for every keyword except "architecture decision" and "model kind".

## 7   Conclusions

In this paper we introduced the results obtained through a feasibility study investigating the mapping of elements from the ISO/IEC 42010 standard [5] on a particularly affirmed and long lived ADL, DARWIN/FSP. From this study we were able to deduce a number of considerations among which:

(i) The presence of consolidated architectural standards and increasing academic interest in its domain is steadily leading to a consensus of terminology and commonly agreed definitions. This means that indeed the standardization effort is having influence on the architecture community. This also suggests that using the 42010 standard as a map is a promising approach to engineer a methodology for our final goal, i.e. leverage architecture relevant information from (technical) ADLs to (standardized) needs of IT practitioners. In this way, alignment of enterprise architecture and software/IT architecture is facilitated;

(ii) There is still little or no recognition for the need of architecturally descriptive viewpoints targeted to every concern an ADL wants to address; this means that indeed there is the strong need and urge to introduce more and more the concept of "viewpoint" in the picture of ADLs - using it as a key for the separation of concerns and an incentive for the ADL selection process, since it clearly delineates the ADL's targeted concerns;

(iii) ADLs remain promising technologies but lack clarity of vision upon expressing and supporting this promise: ADLs are in fact engineered to narrowly support particular engineering domains but these are often undocumented or

open to interpretation; their concepts are not carefully explored and the inter-
dependencies they carry, are left unexplored;
*(iv)* While ADLs do address architecture design, they still underspecify or dis-
regard reasoning and architecture rationale;
*(v)* The methodology used in the presented case study is able to deliver the pragmatic information we are looking for. With this information it is indeed possible
to draw conclusions on a selected ADL and its compliance to ISO/IEC 42010
and ultimately, its fitness and strengths for selected domains.
These considerations pose grounds for more articulated and broader experimen-
tation to solve the problem stated in Section 3, i.e. offer practitioners with a map
to compare and select an ADL depending on their own needs. Though, the main
question deriving from our problem statement was here only initially explored,
and will require further work to be fully answered.

These initial results, however, suggest that a more thorough and automated
mapping strategy is indeed feasible and its potentials are great. A number of
open paths can be explored from this point:
*(a)* automate the compliance verification of ADLs as well as harvest viewpoints
and concerns from their meta-model; *(b)* assess the effective power of expression
of ADLs as matched against ISO / IEC 42010; *(c)* generalize the conclusions in
this paper to a broader ADL set.

Stemming from the results presented in this paper, our ongoing work is addressing point *(a)*. Updates are being disseminated through the Working Group
on Architecture Viewpoints Repository[4] under the ISO umbrella.

## Acknowledgments

The authors would like to thank Rich Hilliard for his invaluable feedback.

## References

1. Alanen, M., Porres, I.: Difference and union of models. In: Stevens, P., Whittle,
   J., Booch, G. (eds.) UML 2003. LNCS, vol. 2863, pp. 2–17. Springer, Heidelberg
   (2003)
2. Babar, M.A., Lago, P.: Design decisions and design rationale in software architecture. Journal of Systems and Software 82(8), 1195–1197 (2009); Editorial Special
   Issue
3. Cicchetti, A., Di Ruscio, D., Pierantonio, A.: A metamodel independent approach
   to difference representation. Journal of Object Technology 6(9), 165–185 (2007)
4. Clements, P., Bachmann, F., Bass, L., Garlan, D., Ivers, J., Little, R., Nord, R.,
   Stafford, J.: Documenting Software Architectures: Views and Beyond. Addison-
   Wesley, Boston (2003)
5. ISO/EIC consortium. ISO/IEC 42010 (2010), http://www.iso.org
6. Giannakopoulou, D.: Model checking for concurrent software architectures, Ph.D.
   Dissertation, Imperial College, London (1999)

---

[4] www.iso-architecture.org/viewpoints

7. DSE Group. The DARWIN language grammar: BNF, Imperial College Report (1997)
8. Favre, L.: Well-founded metamodeling for model-driven architecture. In: Vojtáš, P., Bieliková, M., Charron-Bost, B., Sýkora, O. (eds.) SOFSEM 2005. LNCS, vol. 3381, pp. 364–367. Springer, Heidelberg (2005)
9. Miller, F.P., Vandome, A.F., McBrewster, J.: Architecture Description Language: Software Engineering, Enterprise Modelling, Programming Language, Software Architecture, Systems Architecture, Technical Architecture. Alphascript Publishing (2005)
10. Hilliard, R.: Knowledge mechanisms in ISO/IEC 42010: keynote. In: IEEE/ACM International Workshop on sharing and reusing architectural knowledge (SHARK), pp. 49–50 (2008)
11. Georgiadis, I.: Design issues in the mapping of the darwin adl to java using rmi as the communication substrate. DSE Group, Imperial College, London (1999)
12. Kramer, J., Magee, J.: Concurrency, State Models & JAVA Programs. John Wiley & Sons, Chichester (2006)
13. Magee, J.: Behavioral analysis of software architectures using ltsa. In: International Conference on Software Engineering (1999)
14. Magee, J., Dulay, N., Eisenbach, S., Kramer, J.: Specifying distributed software architectures. In: 5th European Software Engineering Conference (1995)
15. Ng, K., Kramer, J., Magee, J., Dulay, N.: The software architect's assistant - a visual environment for distributed programming. In: 28th Hawaii International Conference on System Sciences (1995)
16. Kramer, J., Magee, J., Dulay, N.: A constructive development environment for parallel and distributed programs, Technical Report, DSE Group, Imperial College, London (1995)
17. Kramer, J., Magee, J.: Engineering distributed software: a structural discipline (2005)
18. Kruchten, P.: The 4+1 view model of architecture. IEEE Software 12(6), 42–50 (1995)
19. Mazzucchi, M.: Darwin ed fsp, Report presso il Politecnico di Milano (2004)
20. Maier, M.W., Emery, D., Hilliard, R.: ANSI/IEEE 1471 and systems engineering. Syst. Eng. 7(3) (2004)
21. Malavolta, I., Muccini, H., Pelliccione, P., Tamburri, D.A.: Providing architectural languages and tools interoperability through model transformation technologies. IEEE Trans. Software Eng. 36(1) (2010)
22. Medvidovic, N.: A classification and comparison framework for software architecture description languages. IEEE Transactions on Software Engineering 26, 70–93 (1996)
23. Mens, T.: A state-of-the-art survey on software merging. IEEE Trans. Softw. Eng. 28(5), 449–462 (2002)
24. Rozanski, N., Woods, E.: Software Systems Architecture: Working with Stakeholders Using Viewpoints and Perspectives. Addison-Wesley Professional, Reading (2005)
25. OMG. Meta Object Facility (MOF) Core Specification Version 2.0 (2006)
26. Rozanski, N., Woods, E.: Applying viewpoints and views to software architecture (2004), http://www.viewpoints-and-perspectives.info
27. Zarvic, N., Wieringa, R.: An integrated enterprise architecture framework for business-IT alignment. In: Pigneur, Y., Woo, C. (eds.) BUSITAL. CEUR Workshop Proceedings, vol. 237, CEUR-WS.org (2006)

# Integrating Standard Platforms in Heterogeneous IT Landscapes through Service-Oriented EAM

Helge Buckow, Hans-Jürgen Groß, Gunther Piller, Karl Prott,
Johannes Willkomm, and Alfred Zimmermann

SOA Innovation Lab e.V., Workstream SOA and Standard Platforms
c/o Deutsche Post AG, Charles-de-Gaulle-Straße 20,53113 Bonn
info@soa-lab.de, helge_buckow@mckinsey.com,
hans-juergen.gross@daimler.com, gunther.piller@fh-mainz.de,
karl.prott@capgemini-sdm.com, johannes.willkomm@iteratec.de,
alfred.zimmermann@reutlingen-university.de

**Abstract.** The SOA Innovation Lab investigates the use of standard software packages in a service-oriented context. As a result, we present a holistic approach for developing a service-oriented enterprise architecture with custom and standard software packages. It starts on enterprise level with the identification of domains where both the SOA paradigm and standard software are of relevance. Here SOA capabilities of products from different vendors can be evaluated within a new maturity framework SOAMMI. After pre-requisites and dependencies between distributed components are determined, a high-level architecture can be developed. On the basis of use cases and integration patterns this high level architecture can be refined and verified. Besides methods and related artifacts, we present current adoption issues for standard software packages in service-oriented contexts.

## 1 Introduction

The growing complexity of IT landscapes is a challenge for many companies. A large number of standard software packages - mostly extended and modified, individual software solutions, legacy applications, and different infrastructure components - lead to high cost and limited responsiveness to new business requirements. Many companies start enterprise architecture management (EAM) initiatives to tackle this problem. In areas where flexibility and agility are important, SOA is the current paradigm to organize and utilize distributed capabilities. Here, the use of standard software is often a challenge, especially when dealing with services on a fine granular level. Although many vendors of standard software packages advertise that their product is SOA enabled, the adoption of SOA with standard software is still rare.

The use of standard application platforms emerged in many cases from the introduction of ERP systems, aiming to cover all basic business functionalities of a company and integrating those into a more or less closed system. ERP application suites often dominate the enterprise architecture application layer and the associated automation of business processes in a rather monolithic, proprietary way [1]. Disadvantages of standard application platforms include potential difficulties when fitting to

E. Proper et al. (Eds.): TEAR 2010, LNBIP 70, pp. 86–99, 2010.

individual business processes. In addition, their limited agility after first customization provides obstacles for the adaption to changed business needs and flexible product or service extensions [2]. Standard platforms are often limited in scope and less performing as compared to their best of breed or custom developed counterparts. Additionally, the integration with other leading systems may be a serious issue and challenge for open system environments, which need to support end-to-end business processes.

Some of these limitations can be overcome with the help of service-oriented architecture. SOA is an IT architecture paradigm that utilizes services as fundamental, flexible, and interoperable building blocks for both, structuring the business and for developing applications. SOA is a business oriented architecture style, often based on best of breed technology for agnostic business services, delivered by applications in a business-focused granularity [1]. An introduction into fundamental SOA concepts, technologies, and case studies can be found e.g. in [3, 4]. A discussion of current architectural standards for SOA reference models and ontologies, reference architectures, maturity models, SOA modeling profiles, and open standards work related to the topic of SOA governance is provided in [5].

Initially SOA was burdened with hype and inflated expectations. Now it is part of an ongoing discussion about software architecture. The benefits of SOA are recognized, they comprise flexibility, process orientation, time-to-market, and innovation. The adoption of tools and methods for SOA is growing. An overview about the current status of adoption can be found in the SOA Check 2009 [6], an empirical study about the development of current SOA systems in Germany. Reports on the maturity of SOA technology from vendors are provided by various analysts (see e.g. [7, 8, 9]).

SOA takes place on different levels of scope – company-wide or system specific, different levels of time horizon – operatively planned and budgeted projects, projects in a 2-3 year project portfolio. Also SOA usually touches different strategic aspects too. All those dimensions can be addressed in different levels of detail and granularity. We have developed methods and tools for these different perspectives of architecture in order to support companies in developing a service-oriented architecture, which takes advantages of the use of standard software packages as much as possible.

On the strategic level we have developed an approach for the design of a service-oriented enterprise architecture, in which the areas where SOA and standard software package promise high benefits are clearly marked [10]. Besides that, we have built a SOA architecture maturity framework. It allows a comprehensive assessment of the SOA ability of standard platforms and their vendors, covering all dimensions of an enterprise architecture, as e.g. structured in TOGAF [11], ensuring the sustainability of the standard software packages in question.

For the tactical planning and the definition of a project portfolio with an up to three year time horizon, our approach contains methods for mapping SOA services of standard software packages to domain maps.

Last but not least, we provide real life SOA use cases and their corresponding solutions in order to effectively build solution architectures on the operative level. Use cases are combined with integration patterns – including corresponding templates – and a capability map for SOA infrastructure components.

One of our finding is that some disadvantages of standard application platforms remain, even after the extension of classical standard system modules with fine-grained service-oriented access shells. In many cases such services are not self-sustaining and have to be used with their whole package, or need to integrate several complete system modules.

In this paper we give an overview of our method in Section 2. The following sections provide details and sketch corresponding artifacts: Section 3 and 4 summarize the identification of domains, where a combination of SOA and standard software is suitable. In Section 5 we introduce a SOA Architecture Maturity Framework. SOA use cases, integration patterns are sketched in Section 6.

## 2 Method Overview

In order to identify areas for the use of standard software packages in a service-oriented environment, it is necessary to establish basic EAM capabilities. This includes the definition of a domain map and a picture of the current IT architecture landscape as the core artifacts for EAM. To develop these artifacts, the role of an enterprise architect needs to be established, who is able to understands business needs and translate them into IT requirements. Finally, governance processes need to be introduced to ensure that the target architecture will be implemented.

The central artifact for developing a SOA landscape is the domain map. The SOA Innovation Lab has developed a method for the creation of domain maps, which is explained in detail in Section 3. We have developed a taxonomy and templates for describing domains and have started to collect best practice examples from members of the SOA Innovation Lab. Each domain map is highly individual, suiting a specific business context. Nevertheless, our collection of domain maps can be used as a starting point for the development of templates for specific industries.

SOA has strong benefits, like agility, flexibility, and reduction of redundancies. These benefits are not a priority in all functional areas - some require efficiency and reliability instead, e.g. HR or Controlling. This means, there is a need to develop cases for SOA and standard platforms based on individual domain requirement, e.g. sales order management. Therefore, the next step is to assess and weight business needs on domain level, as outlined in Section 4. We have developed principles for this weighting of domains. As a result, one can define for each domain whether a solution should be SOA enabled.

For a domain with a business need for the benefits that SOA might offer, it has to be assessed if a SOA enabled standard package is available as a solution. In order to identify packages that might suffice, we have developed a questionnaire to evaluate the SOA ability of a vendor. This questionnaire is based on a SOA architecture maturity framework which we introduce in Section 5. It is constructed by integrating different analysis views, using a consistent meta-model approach based on correlation analysis of intrinsic model elements. For this purpose we have transformed CMMI [12], which is originally an assessment framework for software processes, into a framework to analyze systematically enterprise architectures for packaged based SOA environments. Hereby we have used assessment criteria, maturity domains, architecture capabilities, and level rankings from different SOA maturity models [13]. Additionally we have selected architecture elements from state of art architecture frameworks like TOGAF [11], Essential [14], and Quasar Enterprise [15].

In addition to the overall SOA ability, it is necessary to map the vendor solution to the detailed domain map, to evaluate the overall functional fit. The SOA ability of the identified package then needs to be evaluated against specific SOA use cases. We have constructed a taxonomy for SOA use case descriptions which span functional as well as non-functional characteristics, like performance, transaction volume, security. A short introduction is given in Section 6.

Once a functional fit has been verified, it is necessary to identify dependencies of the standard software package regarding processes, functions and data. For most standard software packages, the deployment unit is not a small collection of tightly coupled services, but rather large bundles of services. In some cases the whole package is required in order to use only few services.

For standard software packages that fulfill the functional and non-funcional requirements, a first draft of the to-be architecture then needs to be developed. This includes the high-level system architecture, as well as integration patterns for the physical architecture (see also [16, 17]). We have developed a capability map for integration that allows, to structure corresponding requirements. In addition, a taxonomy for integration patterns has been constructed and a set of best practices for integration in a SOA environment has been compiled. These patterns can be used to assess the integration capability of a standard software package.

The final step is to define the roadmap for the implementation of the SOA enabled standard software packages. The as-is architecture needs to be evaluated against the target architecture. In many cases a number of standard software packages are already in place, but are not used in a SOA enabled way. The gap between as-is and target architecture then needs to be identified and business cases have to be developed, to prioritize the steps of the implementation.

## 3 Definition of Domain Map

When developing enterprise architecture under the SOA paradigm, a domain map is the central artefact, which structures and organizes the needed capabilities. It uses – from a business point of view – the principles of information hiding, separation of concerns, and tight/lose coupling, and makes them transparent. Since one major goal of SOA is the increase of reusability and flexibility by respecting these principles in business and IT, domain maps provide the corresponding topographic base. Methods for the identification of domain maps are described in several publications, e.g. [15]. Figure 1 shows a typical result.

However, more work needs to be done, if an architect wants to identify areas, where SOA and the use of standard software packages make sense. Here we have introduced the following steps for refinement:

**1) Define degree of differentiation and sharing:** In this step an architect evaluates on domain level the need for differentiation and the ability to be shared throughout the company. This investigation will result in a categorization of the domains and the corresponding capabilities as shown in Figure 2.

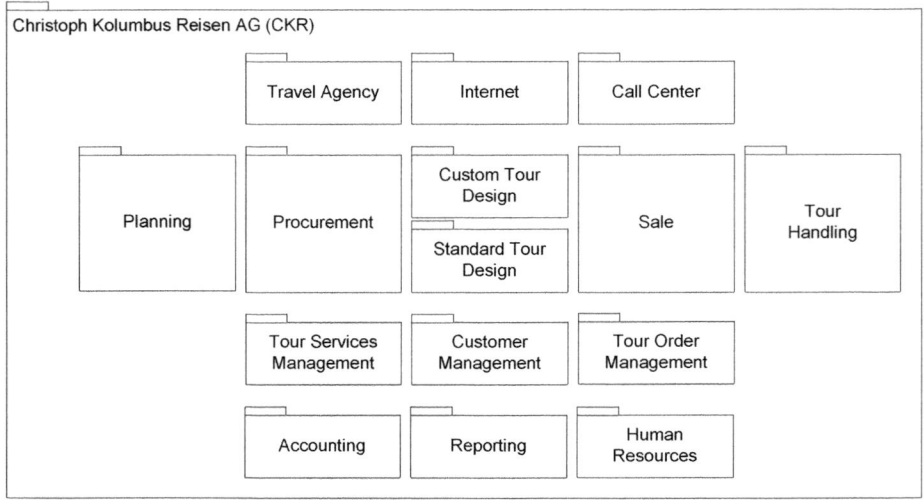

**Fig. 1.** Illustration of a domain map from [15]

**2) Refine domains:** In this step the architect will apply domain refinement patterns to the classified domain map. They are based on the method for finding domains from the SOA Innovation Lab.

**Modularisation:** Here one domain is split into two. This pattern is often applied to domains where the need for differentiation cannot be clearly marked. For example, some capabilities in one domain might have high needs for differentiation, others not. In this case modularisation can make sense, because the IT systems that automate the two different service types are often subject to competing non-functional require-ments, e.g. high flexibility versus cost efficiency

**Generalisation:** This pattern is applied to domains that have some, but not all capa-bilities in common. The common capabilities are generalized and form a new, central-ized domain. They now can be used in a shared way. This situation appears often in domains that cover the same functional area but modularisation has taken place be-cause of a few, e.g. organization or product specific, non-sharable capabilities.

**Aggregation:** This pattern is usually applied to a number of domains that share their low need for differentiation. Here two or more domains are merged. In this case the architect reduces potentially unnecessary complications due to needless loose coupling.

**3) Finalization:** During the whole process of defining a domain map, the stakeholders from business and IT needed to be deeply involved. In addition to this, the architect will have produced different versions of domain maps. In this final step he will need to consolidate the different versions and get a final buy-in for his suggestion.

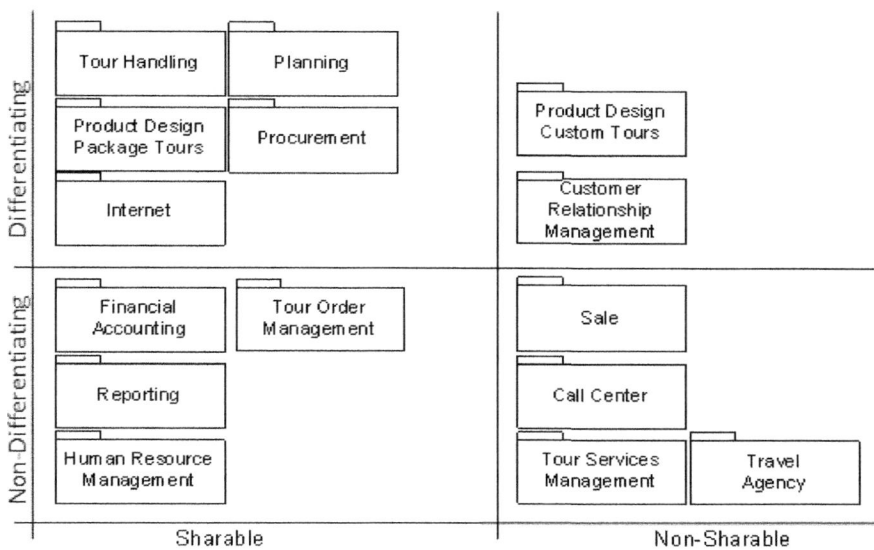

**Fig. 2.** Illustrative example for categorizing domains and their capabilities

## 4   Weight Business Needs on Domain Level

Once an architect has defined a domain map as described above, he will need to characterise the domain map and provide information on a more fine-grained level. The goal is to develop a to-be architecture, which marks clearly those areas where the usage of standard software packages makes sense. In order to achieve this, the architect needs to classify each domain according to its *business needs*, in addition to the need for differentiation and ability to be shared. Figure 3 gives an example for this categorization.

In Figure 3 the columns *sales planning, sales processing* and *sales delivery* are the subdomains of the domain *sales*. Let us illustrate the principle behind these ratings with few examples: For the domain *sales processing,* the business need for *need for differentiation* was rated high, since it is in our example crucial for gaining advantages over competitors to have unique business processes, which assure the shortest throughput times and the best adherence to delivery dates. Because of this, processes must be changed according to changed market requirements and products as quickly as possible – the underlying IT systems must be agile.

For the domain *sales delivery*, we rated the *need for differentiation* and *agility* low. Since, in our example, it would make only little difference whether the corresponding processes were performed similar to those of the competitors or not. Furthermore, these processes have not changed much in the last years and probably will not change in the years to come.

For the latter there is a high potential to use a standard software package in a service-oriented way sustainably - if a package can be found, which automates the needed functionality appropriately.

| Business Needs | Sales Planning | Sales Processing | Sales Delivery |
|---|---|---|---|
| (1) Need for Differentiation | • H | • H | • L |
| (2) Agility | • M | • H | • L |
| (3) Compliance | • M | • H | • H |
| (4) Ability to be reused | • L | • M | • L |
| (5) Business Criticality | • M | • H | • M |

H (High)
M (Medium)
L (Low)

**Fig. 3.** Illustrative Example for categorizing subdomains according to their business needs

For the former the architect will have to do some refinement in order to identify areas on more fine-grained level, where the service-oriented usage of standard software packages makes sense. He will have to identify subdomains and rate them again.

These refinement and rating steps have to be iterated until either agility and differentiation is of low relevance, or the domains represent capabilities that correspond to exactly one role and one goal. This stop criterion is necessary to control the level of granularity and to limit the complexity of an overall SOA landscape. Automating isolated fine-granular services with standard software usually will not bring additional benefits, because dealing with built-in dependencies of standard software package is most often more expensive than automating these services in a custom-built way.

After the architect has iterated through these steps, he will have to identify concrete standard software packages for those domains, for which agility and differentiation are of low relevance. On this basis the architect will develop a to-be architecture, in which fine-grained services on function or data level enhance the standard software packages with needed functionality and where standard software packages offer services that can be combined to higher-level processes. A typical architecture for combining custom and standard software in a service-oriented way is shown in Figure 4.

This architecture is based on the *Application Landscape Reference Architecture* from [15]. It suggests that in an ideal SOA, components should only automate services of exactly one category – interaction, process, function or data – and that the latter should not depend on the former in terms of interface relationships. When dealing with standard software, additional aspects are important:

- Try to avoid the integration of complex custom processes components into standard software components, because this would lead to a significant loss in flexibility, when the custom software components need to be changed. (see (1) in Fig. 4)

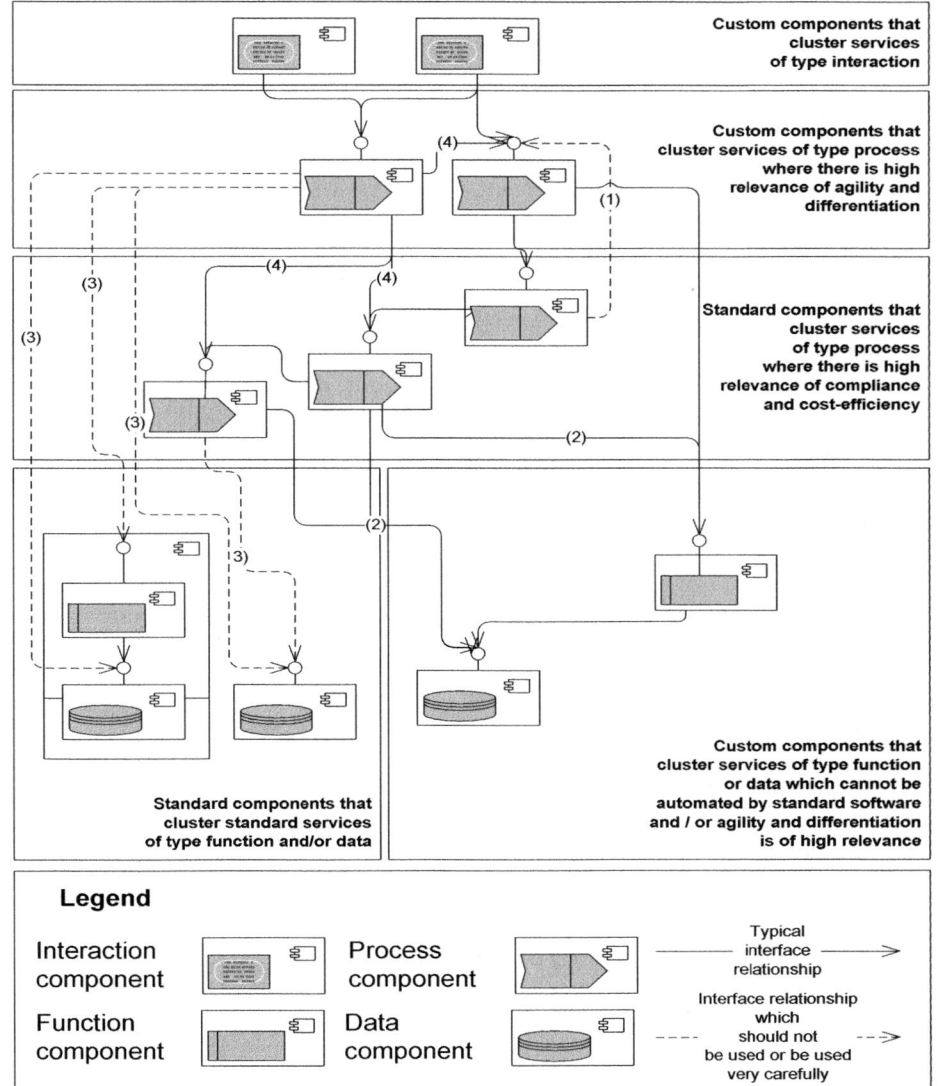

**Fig. 4.** Typical architecture for combining custom and standard software in a service-oriented way

- Missing isolated functionality in standard software components should be added through a service-oriented integration of custom function and data services. Be careful when integrating functionality of higher complexity. (see (2) in Fig.4)
- Try to avoid custom specific relationships to standard software packages if the latter are solely used for isolated function or data services, because the management of those standard software components and the analysis of interdependencies will usually be very time consuming and error prone. (see (3) in Fig.4)

- Combine custom software and standard software processes to higher level processes on the basis of custom built software. (see (4) in Fig.4)

## 5 SOA Architecture Maturity Framework

After domains have been identified, where the use of SOA and standard software is favorable, it has to be checked, if an appropriate standard software package is available. For this purpose, the SOA Innovation Lab has developed the SOA architecture maturity framework SOAMMI [18]. SOAMMI is built upon the metamodel of CMMI and integrates frameworks and architecture standards from various sources: We have included model specific architecture elements from TOGAF and Essential [11, 14]. In addition, we have used assessment criteria, maturity domains, architecture capabilities, and level rankings from state-of-the-art SOA maturity models [13]. The result for the metamodel of SOAMMI is shown in Figure 5.

SOAMMI contains five Maturity Levels [18], where currently most platforms are expected to be located within level one and three:

Maturity Level 1: Initial

- Vendor service architecture is not performed or contains initial coverage only
- Architecture is unpredictable and poorly controlled
- Initial service architecture methods and corresponding knowledge transfer only

Maturity Level 2: Managed

- Vendor service architecture is managed, with medium completeness and coverage
- Vendor supports architecture enablement, corrective actions when necessary
- Vendor service architecture is institutionalized within own products

Maturity Level 3: Defined

- Vendor service architecture is defined with large completeness and coverage
- Customer service architecture is agile, derived from standard vendor architecture
- Vendor supports service strategy and architecture governance with methods, tools

The top level structure of SOAMMI is organized by five architecture domains adapted from TOGAF [11]: Architecture Strategy and Management, Business Architecture, Information Architecture, Application Architecture, Technology Architecture, Service & Operation Architecture, Architecture Realization.

Architecture areas where taken primarily from TOGAF [11], Quasar Enterprise [15] and Essential [14], supplemented by input from realistic integration scenarios from SOA Innovation Lab members. Architecture areas relate to specific goals and specific practices – as known from CMMI [12]. In analogy to CCMI we have also formulated capability levels, generic goals and practices, which demonstrate the institutionalization of specific goals belonging to an architecture area.

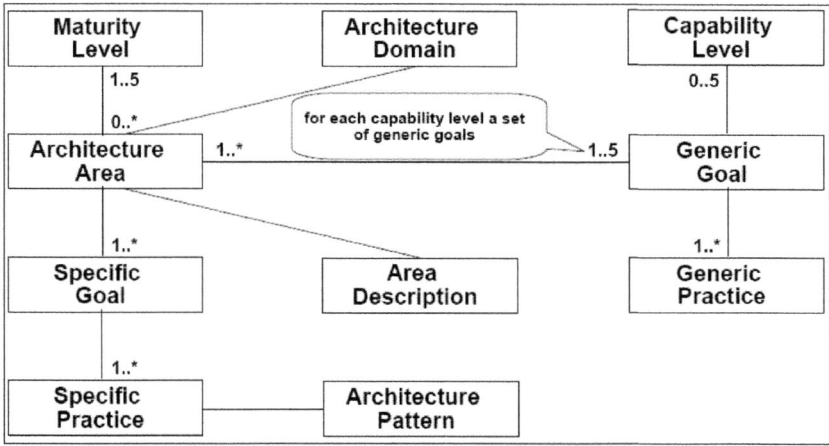

**Fig. 5.** Metamodel of SOA architecture maturity model SOAMMI [18]

As an example, within the architecture domain *Business Architecture* we have the architecture area *Business Capabilities and Services*, which includes specific goals (SG) and practices (SP) like:

- SG: Determine business services for SOA packaged software solutions and optimize business processes
- SP1: Identify and map business services to business capabilities
- SP2: Determine degree of coupling between services

SOAMMI serves as a top-down approach, which ensures that an evaluation of standard software platforms covers all relevant dimensions. For practical assessment workshops with vendors we have combined SOAMMI with bottom-up questions, derived mainly from requirements based on use case scenarios from SOA Innovation Lab members. At the end we have obtained a questionnaire which is structured according to SOAMMI, i.e. specific goals and practices are related to practical assessment questions. As an example, an assessment question for the specific practice *Determine degree of coupling between services* is: *Which are the interdependencies between services and process components?* As a result, a pragmatic questionnaire has been derived, which can be completed in a 3-4 hour workshop with vendor experts. General observations after the assessment of first vendor platforms are:

- Until now only few big implementation projects for SOA and standard software platforms have been realized.
- SOA is clearly embedded in the strategy of most vendors of standard software.
- SOA is often used to provide service-oriented access to data and information of standard software packages.
- Currently SOA is rarely used to break-up and disentangle different components of standard software packages.
- Methods and concepts for the implementation and governance of SOA with standard software are mostly available.

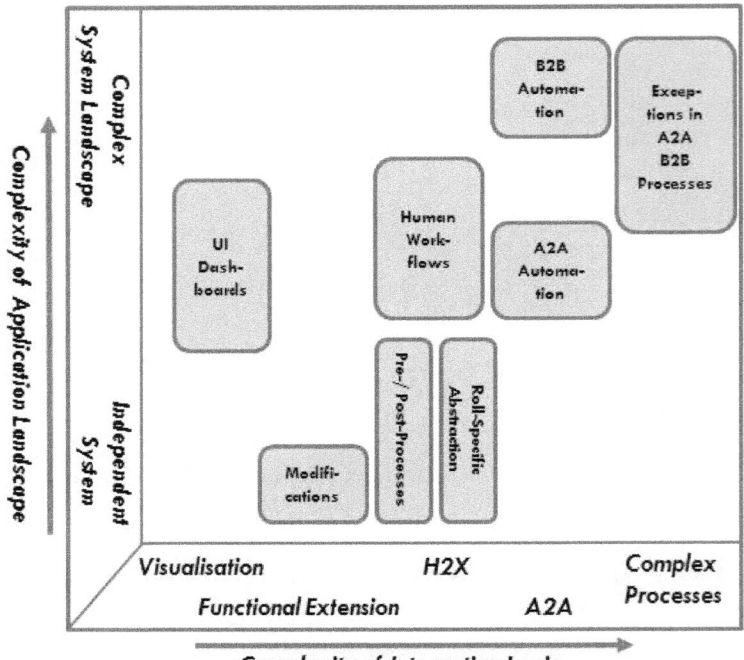

**Fig. 6.** SOA use cases types

# 6  Use Cases and Integration Patterns

Once an overall SOA ability has been verified, a detailed evaluation of SOA use cases needs to be performed. To this end the SOA Innovation Lab has identified important characteristics of SOA use cases and developed a template for use case descriptions. In Figure 6 we show typical types of SOA use cases, distinguished by the complexity of the integration logic and underlying application landscape. A meaningful description of SOA use cases includes a sketch of the system landscape and an application architecture. On integration topics - spanning the integration of front-ends, processes, application logic, and data - detailed information is required. Finally, a use case template also should include a business case summary, as well as benefits and challenges expected from an implementation with SOA.

Integration patterns provide building blocks for the architecture of SOA use cases. The SOA Innovation Lab has developed a template for the description of these patterns. The template consists of five parts: an overview, a problem description with example, a solution proposal. For details see [19].

When identifying an initial pattern catalog the SOA Innovation Lab members recognized two triggers: The first comes from analyzed use cases. For example, one common use case is that end-to-end processes span several departments, users, roles and especially different applications. Some of these applications are customized

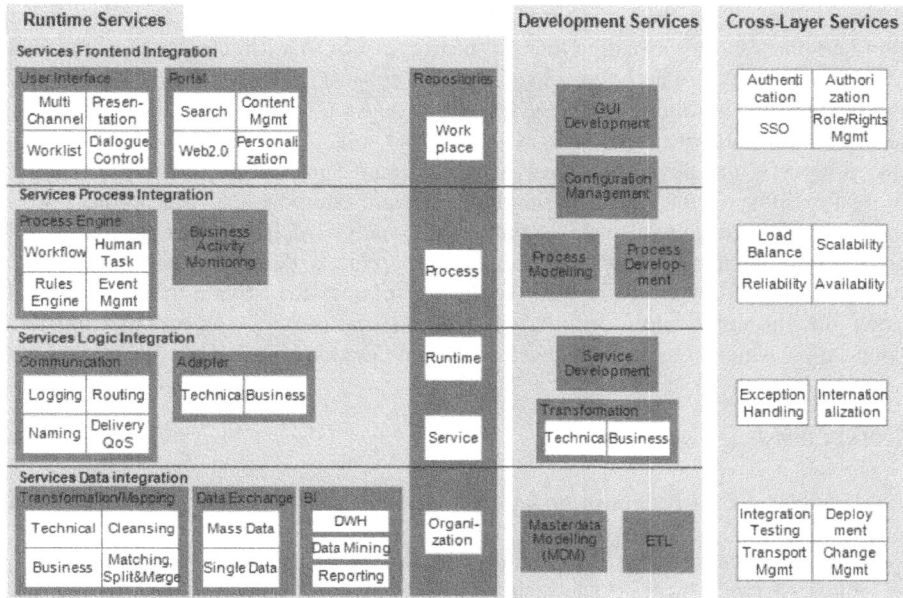

**Fig. 7.** Capability Map – reference architecture for service-oriented integration

standard software packages, others are individual solutions. An often used integration pattern for implementing an IT-based flexible end-to-end process is to encapsulate all involved applications into a common service façade. The service façade manages the access to common data for different software packages and offers one common technical and business interface. In this way the SOA Innovation Lab members derived the service façade as one of the first best practices when combining standard and individual software packages in a service oriented manner.

A second source for integration patterns are technical integration components for SOA implementations: For the physical realization of use cases the SOA Innovation Lab has created a capability map. It has been developed as reference architecture for the service-oriented integration of software components. It contains all integration components needed in SOA implementations (see Figure 7). One component is a service repository. It is common sense that there should be only one logical instance of an enterprise service repository (ESR). Unfortunately each vendor or solution provider introduces his own physical instance of an ESR. So there is need for an integration pattern how to combine all physical instances of an ESR into one logical instance. In this way the capability map becomes a second trigger for further integration patterns.

## 7 Outlook

In this paper we have sketched a holistic approach for developing a service-oriented enterprise architecture with custom and standard software packages. Besides a description of the method, we have introduced important artifacts. The SOA Innovation Lab plans further investigations on the usage of SOA within an EAM framework.

One area of future activities deals with the construction of software landscapes in the context of monolithic business applications. As a result, we will obtain solution proposals for software landscapes with standard software packages and SOA. Part of this project is the development of a requirement catalogue for vendors, aiming at more flexibility in the usage of standard software components. Furthermore we intend to detail our general results related to domain modelling and road mapping for complex application landscapes. Here the systematic development of architecture principles in a SOA world is key. Finally, we plan to investigate methods and solutions for the integration of internal and external services in mixed application landscapes, which consist of on-premise and on-demand solutions.

## References

1. Grigoriu, A.: An Enterprise Architecture Development Framework. Trafford Publishing (2007)
2. CSC: Standardsoftware und geschäftliche Flexibilität. Foundation Bericht 107 (1996)
3. Erl, T.: Service Oriented Architecture. Prentice-Hall, Englewood Cliffs (2005)
4. Krafzig, D., Banke, K., Slama, D.: Enterprise SOA. Prentice-Hall, Englewood Cliffs (2005)
5. Kreger, H., Estefan, J.: Navigating the SOA Open Standards Landscape around Architecture (2009),
   http://www.adobe.com/devnet/livecycle/pdfs/soa_standards.pdf
6. Martin, W., Eckert, J.: SOA Check 2009. Ergebnisse einer empirischen Studie (2009),
   http://www.soa-forum.de/pdf/SOA-check2009.pdf
7. Natis, Y.V., Pezzini, M., Thompson, J., Iijima, K., Sholler, D.: Magic Quadrant for Application Infrastructure for New Systematic SOA Application Projects. Gartner Research 2008 (2009),
   http://www.gartner.com/DisplayDocument?doc_cd=163409
8. Pezzini, M., Natis, Y.V., Iijima, K., Sholler, D., Thompson, J., Vecchio, D.: Magic Quadrant for Application Infrastructure for SOA Composite Application Projects Gartner Research 2008 (2009),
   http://www.gartner.com/DisplayDocument?doc_cd=163401
9. Kenney, F.L., Plummer, D.C.: Magic Quadrant for integrated SOA Governance Technology Sets. Gartner Research 2009 (2009),
   http://www.gartner.com/DisplayDocument?doc_cd=166481
10. Buckow, H., Groß, H.-J., Piller, G., Prott, K., Willkomm, J., Zimmermann, A.: Method for Service-Oriented EAM with Standard Platforms in Heterogeneous IT Landscapes. In: 2nd European Workshop on Patterns for Enterprise Architecture Management (PEAM 2010), Paderborn 2010. GI-Edition - Lecture Notes in Informatics (LNI), P-160 (2010)
11. TOGAF Version 9. The Open Group Architecture Framework (2009)
12. CMMI for Development. Version 1.2 Carnegie Mellon University, Software Engineering Institute (2006), http://www.sei.cmu.edu/reports/06tr008.pdf (2009)
13. ACMM Architecture Capability Maturity Model, The Open Group (2009); Inaganti, S., Aravamudan,S.: SOA Maturity Model. BP Trends (April 2007),
    http://www.bptrends.com/publicationfiles/04-07
    -ART-The%20SOA%20MaturityModel-Inagantifinal.pdf (2009);

Sonic: SOA Maturity Model,
`http://soa.omg.org/Uploaded%20Docs/SOA/SOA_Maturity.pdf` (2009);
Oracle: SOA Maturity Model,
`http://www.scribd.com/doc/2890015/oraclesoamaturitymodelchea`
`tsheet` (2009). Open Group: OSIMM Maturity Model for SOA (2009),
`http://www.opengroup.org/projects`
`/soa-book/page.tpl?CALLER=faq.tpl&ggid=1319`; IBM: SIMM Services Integration Maturity Model (2009),
`http://www.ibm.com/developerworks/webservices/library`
`/ws-soa-simm`

14. The Essential Architecture Project (2009),
    `http://www.enterprise-architecture.org`
15. Engels, G., Hess, A., Humm, B., Juwig, O., Lohmann, M., Richter, J.P., Voß, M., Willkomm, J.: Quasar Enterprise. Dpunkt.verlag (2008)
16. Fowler, M.: Patterns of Enterprise Application Architecture. Addison-Wesley, Reading (2003)
17. Hohpe, G., Woolf, B.: Enterprise Integration Patterns. Addison-Wesley, Reading (2004)
18. Zimmermann, A.: SOAMMI – SOA Maturity Model Integration - Conceptual Framework (to be published)
19. Prott, K., Wissing, M.: Praxis erprobte Muster und Landkarten zur service-orientierten Integration von Standardsoftware. Submitted to INFORMATIK 2010, Leipzig (2010)

# Author Index

GPSR Compliance

The European Union's (EU) General Product Safety Regulation (GPSR)
is a set of rules that requires consumer products to be  safe and our
obligations to ensure this.

If you have any concerns about our products, you can contact us on
ProductSafety@springernature.com

In case Publisher is established outside the EU, the EU authorized
representative is:

Springer Nature Customer Service Center GmbH
Europaplatz 3
69115 Heidelberg, Germany


**Batch number: 09490872**


Printed by Printforce, the Netherlands